INTRODUCTION TO
PRACTICAL SPIRITUALITY

INTRODUCTION TO PRACTICAL SPIRITUALITY

Selected Lessons from
Archangel Gabriel

Second Edition

Channeled by
Reverend Penny Donovan

Edited by Peter Santos

Sacred Garden Fellowship, Inc.
Albany, New York

Published by Sacred Garden Fellowship, Inc.
Albany, NY
www.sacredgardenfellowship.org

ISBN-13: 978-1932746037

Acknowledgements

This book would not have been possible without the support and efforts of many in the Sacred Garden Fellowship (SGF) community including Donald Gilbert, Virgil McIntosh, Peter Santos, and of course Reverend Penny Donovan. In addition, the contributions of many others in the SGF community have been essential to sustaining SGF and promoting its mission, helping bring the organization to a place where it's possible to bring this book into publication. SGF also offers deep loving gratitude to the nonphysical teachers, guides, and angels who have been there every step of the way, challenging us and offering opportunities for both the organization and the community to grow spiritually, and guiding us ever forward on the path to Truth. And finally, many thanks to the reader who has been drawn to these lessons and is now joined on the path of advancing themselves towards awakening the divinity within.

Table of Contents

Preface

In October of 1987, my life changed very drastically one Sunday. I went to church, as I had done for twenty-three years. As I went into my office to get my Bible and get ready to go up on the podium, I felt very light-headed and dizzy and I thought, "Well, I ate dinner early. Maybe I just need some food." The feeling kind of passed as I went out on the podium.

I remember saying to the congregation, "Before I give my talk, we have a meditation." The last thing I remember was the meditation. The next thing I knew I was standing at the lectern with everyone standing up and applauding! I didn't know what had happened. The people were saying, "It was wonderful! A teacher came."

It was during the next few days that the teacher revealed himself to me as being the Archangel Gabriel. He said, "I will teach you things and if you will follow and do them, they will change your life for the better."

That was the beginning of the twelve years during which he channeled through me, teaching truths and providing spiritual guidance. His teachings were simple, loving. I watched the people in my congregation change, evolve, and grow.

He was challenged many times by me and others, and never did he lose his temper. He never was anything but loving and kind, and he never failed to have an answer to any question that was given to him. He was a very powerful, loving force in my life and in the lives of the people who came to hear him over the years.

People have often asked me what it was like to channel Gabriel and how I felt after he left us for good in 1999. For a long time it was difficult to put into words the feelings I had of the channeling and his leaving. I awoke one morning and the words were there and I share them now with you.

Gabriel was an energy, a divine energy, that overtook my consciousness and my body from an indefinable Source. He was not greater than I, but he was more powerful and strong-willed with an intent of absolute love and goodness. He overrode my fears and caused me to be so still that I seemed to disappear. I was aware of him, bound and consumed in the love of him. My surrender was complete and only in retrospect do I realize how totally I trusted him. Once I surrendered, I never entertained the idea of stopping.

When it was over, I felt an emptiness inside, an emptiness that rises to the surface now and then as a great longing for something lost before time began. Yet at other times the mere memory of him brings a comfort beyond words. It will never be again, yet it will never be totally gone. Gabriel left something of himself that will be with me always, beyond earth or heaven;

an addition to the fabric that is my true self, a gift more pure than mind can comprehend. And so it is.

Reverend Penny Donovan

Introduction

Reverend Penny Donovan is a psychic who has been a natural medium since childhood. She studied under Reverend Edith S. Wendling at the John Carlson Memorial Institute in Buffalo, NY where she was ordained in 1960. She obtained her Doctor of Divinity degree from the Fellowships of the Spirit in Buffalo, NY.

In 1964, she founded the Trinity Temple of the Holy Spirit Church in Albany, NY where she served as pastor for thirty years. To devote more time to the teachings of Archangel Gabriel, in November 1994, she retired as pastor of Trinity Temple and founded Springwell Metaphysical Studies. In January 2005, she established a new organization called The Gabriel Fellowship for the preservation, publication, and teaching of Gabriel's lessons. This organization merged with the Sacred Garden Retreats organization, founded by Donald Gilbert, MSW, in November 2009 to become the Sacred Garden Fellowship (SGF).

SGF makes available audios, books, and booklets of Archangel Gabriel and Rev. Penny's and Don Gilbert's seminars and lectures. The organization also conducts regular meetings to support those who seek spiritual guidance and continued expansion of their knowledge and understanding of spiritual truths. It is SGF's desire that, in all these lessons, the reader finds truths that resonate within and deeply touch their life.

Archangel Gabriel taught for twelve years from October 1987 to December 1999 at evening lectures and all-day seminars, usually one or two times a month but sometimes more often. When he identified himself to Rev. Penny, there was a concern that listeners might become attached to the excitement and drama around the channeling of an archangel and follow or idolize Gabriel or Rev. Penny herself. So, in order to keep the focus on the lessons, Gabriel decided to call himself Lucas in the early lectures.

His talks were primarily given in Albany, New York where Rev. Penny lived. However, she did travel to other locations to provide opportunities for Gabriel to teach different audiences. Most of his seminars and lectures were audio taped, resulting in over 250 recorded sessions.

Over the years, Gabriel's teachings covered a wide spectrum of spiritual truths ranging from the nature of God and who we are as Spirit to our current level of evolvement and spiritual understanding in this physical dimension. He explained how and why we are here on earth, our purpose for being here, and what we must do to return home to our remembrance of our Spirit within.

He covered many topics such as our levels of consciousness, reincarnation, energy, our egos, the power of our thoughts, negative and positive thinking, unconditional love, forgiveness, and the purpose of the experiences we go through in our lives. His central theme was always for us to live our truth through unconditional love, compassion, and forgiveness, and with the knowing that we are truly the Children of God.

As he said he would, Gabriel taught his final lesson in December 1999. Since then, Rev. Penny has continued to present spiritual truths through her writings, classes, and in conjunction with Donald Gilbert, conduct spiritual retreats where she continues to teach and channel master teachers, including Yeshua (the Master Jesus).

Rev. Penny's love of God, her teaching and channeling talents, her ability to incorporate lessons in truth gleaned and developed from a lifetime of spiritual learning and growth, and her desire to help others find their spiritual path and highest good are a gift to us and our world.

After channeling through Rev. Penny for twelve years, Gabriel made it clear that he would not be returning to the earth plane for another two thousand years. However, in May 2015, he made a surprise visit during an SGF weekend retreat that was on the topic of how his material would be taught to others. SGF had put together a first level curriculum of Gabriel's materials—including a video, an introductory book of selected sessions, and a syllabus for a nine-week course—and Gabriel blessed us with his presence to clarify how his wonderful teachings are to be presented.

From his words at that retreat:

The teachings that I have given on the earth plane through this beloved woman are not to be changed in any way. They are to be taught verbatim as it was given. There shall be no interpretation of it, no addition of, "This is important. You don't have to pay attention to that." You are to teach it *word for word*.

If you feel it necessary to give an example to whomever you are teaching, you will say, "These are not Gabriel's words. These are my words. I found a benefit by thinking what he said in this way." But you are not to change one word of what I gave. The reason being... What I gave is pure Truth, absolute pure Truth from the highest there is. It is given to the earth plane in its Truth. It loses value when it is interpreted, when it is dissected, and all this sort of thing.

And later...

Don't interpret what you are transcribing. Transcribe it word for word, even if the language is incorrect.

This volume of unedited transcriptions by Archangel Gabriel contains his words as they were spoken. As such, copyediting to accepted standards such as the *Chicago Manual of Style* was not a

Introduction

priority. Instead, as directed, the text is word for word from the audio recordings, including seeming inconsistencies in grammar.

In addition, care was taken to reflect Gabriel's manner of speaking and emphasis on particular words or phrases. His frequent pauses and recurrent use of "now," "and," and "but" at the beginning of sentences were also retained.

Most of the time, Gabriel's voice comes through the recordings quite strongly and clearly (as he is a powerful speaker) but there are occasional inaudible words or phrases when his voice was softer and/or when the recording did not pick up the sound well. Even though sometimes the inaudible word or phrase seems obvious, it is indicated in the text as "[inaudible]" so the reader can make his or her own decision as to the meaning.

While in Rev. Penny's physical form, Gabriel sometimes jokes around with the group he is teaching. He also occasionally speaks or consults with his playful angel helper, known as Tinkerbell, who has a better understanding of earthly matters than he does and who delights in joking and finding joy in even the smallest of things. These digressions from the lessons are typically included to show his grand and wondrous personality.

This book contains selected teachings from Gabriel's twelve years of lessons and is intended to accompany the SGF course of the same name, although the teachings can certainly stand on their own. The lectures were chosen by Rev. Penny and Don

Gilbert in order to introduce the basic concepts of spiritual understanding that Gabriel taught during his time here.

It is Sacred Garden Fellowship's hope that the reader truly *feels* the teachings contained in this volume and aspires to practice and *live* the lessons as given. This is the first point in SGF's mission; "To encourage all to become aware of and live from their God-Self."

May you be blessed on your journey.

INTRODUCTION TO PRACTICAL SPIRITUALITY

Selected Lessons from
Archangel Gabriel

How We Are Guided

September 13, 1998

Archangel Gabriel: It is wondrous to be here in your little chapel that is being spit and polished, eh? Indeed.

I wish to speak to you tonight on how you are guided, how you receive your information from your spirit helpers, from angels, and also, most importantly, from your higher self. For never are you alone and never are you left on your own to muddle through something, even though sometimes you think that's exactly what is happening. Especially Beloved Woman seems to do that a lot.

The higher self of you...that is the part of you that is directly connected to the personality that you are, that you have put on to use while you are here upon the earth, and that guidance is the purest guidance that you will receive because it is from the Spirit Self of you. Now, that guidance never leaves you. You *think* it does, but when you think it is absent, that is when the personality self of you has so gotten itself so churned up that it is blocking the flow of the intuitive voice of God within you.

3

INTRODUCTION TO PRACTICAL SPIRITUALITY

In order to be aware of the guidance of your higher self, it is important that you become very still, very still. I don't mean just physically still, but it is important that you become mentally still and that you use your centeredness, centering yourself in the light, in the Christ awareness, and allowing yourself to rest in that light.

Now when you do that, the portals of heaven open to you because the Spirit Self of you ever abides in what you would term to be heaven where there is absolute peace, where there is joy, perfect love, perfect everything. And when you are centering yourself to receive from the God Self of you, never are you denied that access, never. You are never turned away. There is no time in which the God of you says, "I don't want to talk to that personality. They have offended me. Therefore, let them go and muddle through." That never happens. When you center yourself, you're bringing into alignment all of the chakras, which is important. You're also bringing in line your mental body, your emotional body, your etheric body, and your physical body, and you are aligning them in perfect order.

Now, this is necessary. Why? Because the God Self of you has to pour into those bodies the awareness of that which it is trying to bring to you, and these bodies are in perfect alignment *when you request that they be*. It's that simple. You don't have to get into any particular position. You don't have to be doing anything. All you have to do is ask, "I ask for complete alignment of my total being," and it is done.

Now, the reason it is done upon request is because you are not always in a position to sit with your spine straight and your feet on the floor and your hands upward. What if you're driving a mode of transportation? Well, you could do it but I think you'd go into a ditch or something, eh? So, in order for this to be ever, ever available to you, it is such that it happens upon request. All you have to do is ask.

Now the thing is that a lot of you, when you get into a muddle over something, you don't think to ask. You say, "Oh God, help me," but you don't think to align yourself so that you are *aware* of the help that is there. You become immediately upset and when you do, you make a zigzag in your alignment instead of it being straight.

Now it only takes a moment, a second of your time, to just think it. "I desire to be in complete alignment." And when you think it, it happens instantly and then the flow of information from the higher self of you comes down without interference, with no interference whatsoever. It is there and it pours in and you become aware of it.

Now, that awareness takes many forms depending on what you are asking for, why you feel in need of it. It can come as a sense of peace. It can come as a sense of being removed from an unbearable situation. It can come as an inspiration of what to do or what to say. It can come as a feeling, "It's all right. Everything is all right. I shall know how to proceed." It comes in accordance with what your request for it is and it never, never not works. It always works for you, ever. It doesn't matter what is going on.

Bringing in the higher self of you...each time you do this... This is the most important way for you to receive guidance because each time you do this, you become more and more open to it, and it happens that it is more readily recognized by you. When you are a stranger to it, frequently it happens and you don't recognize it. It's like asking and asking and the answer is right in front of your face and you keep saying, "Get out of my way. I have to ask a question," and you don't see the answer. But as you are *always* tuned to the higher self of you, the answer when it is there, you *know* it is there. It is not a thing where you think you have not been answered. You *know* it is there.

"Well, if I can do all of that, then what do I need angels for and certainly why do I need master teachers and guides and so forth like that?" you're thinking. We all have our purpose. I wouldn't like to think that you didn't think we had any purpose.

Now, angels work differently than human guides do. We work differently because we are not bound to the earth. We have no vested interest in the earth. We have no vested interest in your physical, material lives. Our interest in you is purely and only spiritual. We care how you are from a spiritual point of view so we work very intimately with your connectedness to the God Self of you.

What you perceive to be a materialistic or a physical concern, we see as an opportunity for you to exercise your Godness. We see this as an opportunity for you to become more and more aware of who you really, really are in terms of your son of Godness. So we are not looking at a situation, a physical situation, from the aspect of how is this going to be physically or materially for you. We look at it as how is it going to be spiritually for you. Are you going to grasp the lesson, recognize its opportunity, and use it? And are you going to use it from the higher self of you?

We watch you have your little moments of higher self-awareness and then we watch you slide off the track, as it were, and get caught in the *appearance* of a material situation. And as you get caught in the appearance of that situation, you feed energy into it and the situation appears to be larger than you and it never is. It never is.

So, when you are tuning in to the higher self of you, you *instantly* have angel help and angels will do whatever the higher self of you is asking for.

Now, what would the higher self ask for, for you? Only your highest good. No matter what the situation is, angels will protect you from unnecessary anything. They will bring in and *hold* when you cannot. They will hold through their vibration the healing, the help, the protection, the love, the blessing and they hold that in place all around you. And whether you realize it or not, the situation, even though it appears difficult to you, becomes less so because we hold that vibration of absolute good around you at all times, all times.

Physical situations are *always* dealt with from a spiritual perspective by angels. Always, without fail. It doesn't matter whether it is an extreme condition or whether it is simply trying to make up your mind whether to go here or go there. It is always looked upon as a spiritual happening because in truth it is a spiritual happening.

INTRODUCTION TO PRACTICAL SPIRITUALITY

If you could know what little bearing your physical lives have from a physical standpoint upon the soul aspect of you, you would understand why we say that every happening is a spiritual happening to you. Everything that happens to you is a spiritual decision. It is a time, an opportunity, for you to choose the spiritual path or to choose to become entangled in appearance, entangled in the energies of what the ego would have you believe. So everything that happens to you is a spiritual choice.

Now you might think, "But some of the things that happen to me are not spiritual at all. They're very earthy. And what about that?" Even that had its beginning in a spiritual idea that you took within yourself for the purpose of the gift it could give you. It brings to you *ever* an opportunity to discover how *powerful* you are spiritually, how truly, truly powerful you are.

Now, some of you think that you are victims of circumstance. "Well, I can't change this person. I can't change that situation because of this person." No. You don't have to change a situation because of another person. You change whatever you change because of you, within yourself and you make that decision from the spiritual aspect of you as to what is the gift, and how you have asked for that gift for you to show your *self*, show your personality, how spiritually powerful you truly are.

As angels, we are never allowed to interfere with your free will, ever. Sometimes it's very difficult for us to stand by and watch you make what we consider to be very poor decisions. But whatever you decide, we

8

are there to support you in it and we will work from the aspect of your spiritual intent, what you have decided from the spiritual higher self of you. In any situation, we are there to support and to guide you and to give you strength and love.

Now there are always certain elements that are involved in any earthly situation. The first element is the opportunity to use your God Self. That is always the first and foremost reason why one chooses certain difficulties...is the opportunity to prove that you are master over it, that you are never a victim, that you are never on the receiving end of...what is it you call it? The very short stick? Short end of the stick? Whatever. You always have the opportunity to use your higher self and that is the first reason.

The second reason is discernment. How do you look at a situation? How do you see what you are into? Do you see it as something fearful, something over which you have no control? Or do you see it as, "I shall walk through this and I shall take from it its blessing, and that is all that I shall take from it"? That is a difficult thing. That is a difficult thing because you are looking at a situation that would *appear* to you to be unbearable or unsolvable or "How can I ever make my way through this?" And yet, regardless of that, the higher part of you is encouraging you...be in tune with your force.

Know you how you had a make-believe story upon your picture boxes about traveling through space and meeting monsters and all that sort of thing and the key phrase through that was, "May the force be with you." Remember that? You are always with the force with you. That is a very fine blessing to wish upon another, "May the force be with you." But in situations, you have to go within yourself and know the force, the power of your Spirit. Now, when you do that, angel help comes in instantly, for that's what we're there for. We come and we hold that vibration of spirituality around you and we see you through every bit of it.

The other aspect that is so very important and that a lot of people don't even look at is forgiveness. When you are in a difficulty, it usually involves another person, or sometimes more than one person, and your tendency to blame rises up very strongly, the tendency to see the other fellow as the reason why you are in the mess you're in and to not recognize that that individual—or many individuals, whatever you are dealing with—they are there doing exactly what you requested of them, and that is a very hard lesson, a very hard lesson.

Look at your antagonists, for they are mirroring to you the lesson you asked for. You think, "No way. Nope, nope, nope. I can't accept that. I would *never* ask these people to treat me so poorly. I would *never* do that. I would... No way." Oh yes, you do. Why do you? First of all, most of you believe you deserve it, but more importantly, you are asking, "Dear God, help me to know how strong I am. Help me to know the power that I have as the child of God. Help me to love my antagonist and to forgive them for what appears to be to me something unforgivable. And in that forgiveness, Father, allow me to understand that they have given to me the gift I asked of them."

Now, that is a difficult thing. That is extremely difficult because nobody wants to be in a hard place, and everyone wants to think they got there accidentally or because of another person's mistake. And the truth being that you are always in your hard places because that is what you have chosen.

Now, when you reach into that forgiveness, what is going on? First of all, there's nothing to forgive the person for because they only gave you what you asked them to. So where does this forgiveness come? Why would one need to ask forgiveness? Because you are asking for yourself. You are asking for your own forgiveness. And since it is nearly impossible for the average human being to look at their own need, by personality standards, to be forgiven, you always project it outward onto someone else or something else...a situation, if not a person.

So, when you are forgiving, what are you doing? You are recognizing that first of all, this is a gift, a wondrous gift, and I, in recognizing the gift, recognize that forgiveness is the releasing and letting go of every error perception that I held that caused me to draw this to me in the first place. It is a form of cleansing, of releasing, of letting go, of getting rid of all of the debris that you pulled to you, that drew this very thing that you hated so to you. So you are cleansing. You are releasing and letting go of every error perception that you held about yourself that would have made you draw to you a painful situation.

Secondly...or thirdly or fourthly, wherever we are...because forgiveness is part of an error perception, when you forgive, you come up out of that realization when you truly forgive. Now, forgiveness is a funny thing. It can wear many faces. You can say, "Oh, I forgive them. I'll never forget what they've done, but I forgive them." If you can't forget it, then you haven't forgiven.

Now, is this to say that no matter what happens, you say, "Oh, I forgive them. That was nothing. Nope. I'm fine"? No, it's not. You honor your pain. It's your pain. It's real to you. It's something that is a distressful thing. You don't just say, "Oh, it didn't happen. It's all right." That's not forgiveness. That's burying something.

Forgiveness is when you recognize a thing has happened to you. You recognize that you asked for it for its gifts and you recognize that whoever is involved with it is there because you invited them, and you recognize that in the forgiveness, you are cutting the bonds that held them to you. You are releasing them and you are releasing yourself from this whole thing. And you are allowing the child of God of you to come out into the sunlight and play because there is nothing dark about you any longer. You have released it and let it go.

Do you forget it? In the terms of constantly talking about it and drawing it back to you, yes, you do forget it. Do you forget it inside of you? No. You remember the blessing. You remember the lesson. And every time you think about it, you bless everyone involved in it and you thank them for their gift. Now, as you do this, what happens to the guidance part? Your guidance opens up wide. Why? Because you have taken away the barriers that closed it off.

Some of you wonder when something happens to you, why weren't you told about it ahead of time? Why weren't you warned? In this world full of psychics why didn't somebody tell you? Because some things you have to walk through in order to realize the value of what it is. Some things you can read about happening to someone else and you learn from it, but some things have to be on a one-to-one basis for you to get the impact of what is really being taught.

And when those times are, no one is going to warn you or tell you about it ahead of time because we're not allowed to. You have asked for this lesson. Hard as it be, you have asked for it, and we can be there to love you through it, to guide you, to protect you, to help you, to strengthen you, but we are not allowed to stop it. We are there to pick up the pieces afterward but we cannot prevent it from happening.

Spirit guides and teachers work on a very different level than angels and on an extremely different level than your higher self. People are people. *Ever are they people.* It doesn't make any difference how long you go, how far you go in your climb in your evolution, you still are people. Is that bad? Well, it depends upon where you are sitting, I guess! But no, it isn't bad.

People guides guide you from their own perspective of how they would deal with the same situation if they were in your place. Now that puts a whole other...what is your word? Whole other spin on it because now you are engaging in the assistance of an advisor who looks at things very much from the same perspective that you do.

Ah, I see some of you thinking, "Oh, no." But it's a grand truth. Does that make them invalid as helpers? Not at all. Not at all. Sometimes it takes one to help one. Sometimes it takes a person to help a person. An angel doesn't know how you feel but another person would. Another person would have an understanding of your situation that an angel wouldn't have. They would see it, could look at it, from the perspective of your pain or your discomfort. And in that way, because it is not their pain and not their discomfort, like a good and trusted friend, they can offer you very solid advice because they know how you feel, but they are not entangled in it so they can have an objective viewpoint, which is very valuable. Because they will often point things out to you that an angel would not because an angel wouldn't see it from that same level at all. So there is much to be said for the guidance of people guiding people, very much to be said for it.

And you always attract guides to you that would be of help. You never attract someone to you that wouldn't know what to do in your situation, ever. You always have those who are helpful. And you always have those who have an interest in what you do. They're interested in it because either they did it or they always wanted to or they are somehow drawn to it for that reason.

How do all of these things work together? Beautifully. We never get in each other's way and that's something you can't say! (Laughter) Angels know when to back off and let people help. People know when to call upon the angels to help you. And your own internal higher self *always* knows which kind of help and which kind of guidance that you need the most at the moment and that's the kind that is sent to you, ever, always, without exception.

I don't know your time here. Are we over time? This is fine? All right. When I need to shut up, poke me. (Laughter) I'm used to going all day, you know, so...five more minutes? All right.

The higher self of you brings in your God awareness—the *power*, the *power* that you have as a spiritual being—and you are extremely powerful. The angels come in and they work with that spiritual power. They assist you in that.

People guides and teachers come in and they work for you from the reasoning mind of you, from the earthy, thinking type of mind of you. And all of these things dovetail one into the other to fit perfectly. And when that happens, no matter what your situation is, everything works to your highest good because it takes you up out of it and into a broader scope where you can see and look and *know* all of the nitsy-gritsies about it.

Some of you are in situations that are not extreme but are very annoying. Well, I guess that would be true of just about everybody in the room at some point. You get into situations that are very annoying and you have to deal with them on a daily basis, some of you. What happens then? Then you call upon the higher self of you, "Let me see this through the eyes of love. Let me know this through the eyes of understanding and give me strength." And this will give you a different perspective on the whole situation.

And remember, at any point you can change your mind and do something different. At any point you can take your life into [inaudible] control from your higher self and you can heal yourself. You can allow freedom to come where you felt confined or limited. You can allow a depth of understanding that you never had before. And it's there for the asking. All you have to do is ask for it and it is there.

And on that note, I shall sit me down.

Participant: Do we serve as healing guides for each other and this planet? In other words, do people come to give each other lessons?

Gabriel: Oh, indeed. Indeed, you do. The guides I was referring to are people who have passed into spirit and have chosen to work as a guide to help others, but people interacting with people in the third dimension...yes, they do help, very much so. Very much.

Any others? We've got dead air here. (Laughter) Goodness...no questions at all? Must be you all got it, eh? You always have a question...you have none tonight? Isn't that amazing!? (Laughter) My, how she's grown. Any others?

Participant: Beloved Gabriel, you spoke tonight about the power of forgiveness...

Gabriel: Indeed.

Participant: ...mostly from the viewpoint of forgiving others who we may have perceived as doing wrong to us. Can you say anything about situations where you may have felt the opposite?

Gabriel: Where you feel guilty or something? That perhaps is the most difficult type of forgiveness because one generally judges oneself more harshly than one judges another. But even in that, remember, most people do the best they can at the moment with the highest good of intent. Most people do. Now, there are exceptions to that.

Ask yourself what prompted you to do whatever it is you think you have done and if given the same situation this day in your time, would you do it again? And when you get the answer, then you will know how much you have forgiven yourself. And releasing it and letting it go.

Participant: In a situation of forgiveness, I can...how do I say this? A situation occurs and I can't find it within myself to forgive. Now, I'm all right with that in the sense that I can just turn it to God and just say to God, "You have to take care of this because I can't right now," and I'm fine with that and I know God's all right so that's fine. But I know eventually, somehow, I'm going to have to see this face. I don't know how to do that.

Gabriel: First of all, beloved entity, recognize that in saying to God, "I can't forgive now. Forgive *for* me," you are inviting the highest...your higher self to work through this situation. When you do that, that higher self comes in and it will present to you a little here, a little there, a little here, a little there...avenues to forgive a lesser thing.

Participant: I've had a lot of that!

Gabriel: But beloved entity, don't you see that in practicing the little things of forgiveness, you reach a point where after a bit, you come to recognize that there really isn't anything to forgive. You come to that point and when you come to that point, then the thing that you thought you could *never* forgive, you *do* forgive. You let go. But you have to do the little steps...the little steps.

And the other thing, beloved entity, when you are seeking to forgive something that has not allowed you, by your perception, to defend or protect and therefore something that you treasured was stolen or hurt, one of the reasons that you find it difficult to forgive is because you are blaming yourself, and that is the part, really, that must be looked at and released and let go of.

Participant: In that same vein, when something has occurred and you have forgiven the person involved, but it doesn't occur to you until many years later that the part that still is connected there is...all of a sudden you realize you haven't forgiven yourself for your stupidity and your part in it.

Gabriel: Your what?

Participant: (Laughter) Error perception.

Gabriel: Better. (Laughter) Beloved woman, all forgiveness has to do with the self, all forgiveness. Even though it *appears* to you that you need to forgive somebody out here, ultimately you recognize that you agreed to participate in whatever it was that happened, and you can look at it and you can think, "Why did I ever do that? That was so dumb of me. Why would I have wanted to participate in something like that?" And then the blame comes, like a wave that goes backwards, it comes back on you and you think, "I should have *never* gotten involved. I should have never *allowed* this. I should have never agreed to participate." And when you start thinking like that, you are blaming yourself, and self-forgiveness is very difficult. People can easily forgive another quicker than they can forgive themselves. But there is where you have to say, "Dear God, I can't love me right now. I can't love me, but You can love me and hold me in love until I can love myself again. And help me to love myself again."

Participant: It would seem to me that, if we're talking about forgiveness, that maybe it's a good idea to get in the habit of forgiving all the time...

Gabriel: Oh, indeed it is.

Participant: ...and not wait until there's something that we think we have to forgive?

Gabriel: But sometimes, beloved woman, it takes a mountain before you recognize that you had been walking over the hills without forgiving.

Participant: This is true, and this is why maybe it's just a good idea to just forgive even if we don't *think* there's anything that needs to be forgiven. If we are all carrying a sense of wrongness about us, how can it possibly hurt to forgive ourselves and to forgive others all the time without it being a big deal.

Gabriel: It doesn't hurt to forgive at all, at any point, for anything, under any circumstances, but there are not many people who see the need for forgiveness.

Example: You are driving your mode of transportation and someone cuts in front of you and you curse at them (I don't mean *you* do) or you wish a bad thing, "Well, I hope you get yours," or "Someday, you'll learn," or something of that sort and you forget about it. It doesn't occur to you at that moment to say, "All right, I don't like what that person just did. It made me angry, but I choose not to go there. I choose to take the higher road. I choose to forgive him and to wish them well." Little things like that.

Participant: Sure, it's like most people would say that they should exercise, but maybe if they'd start by walking from the sofa to the TV, they get a little habit and then they get around the block.

Gabriel: Or park further away from the ice cream parlor, where you have to walk. (Laughter) Indeed.

Participant: If you have someone or you know of someone who had a specific expertise in some area and you may or may not have known this person on earth, can you ask for their help?

Gabriel: Oh, indeed you can.

Participant: And you'll get it.

Gabriel: If they themselves don't come—'cause they have free will, you know—they will ask someone else to come that they feel confident could give you the same amount of help.

Participant: Gabriel, how do you handle wanting to share something that you love dearly and having it not accepted at all?

Gabriel: Know you how it tells you in Scripture not to cast your pearls before the swine? And I'm not name calling.

Participant: Thank God for that! (Laughter)

Gabriel: But when you love something and you want to share it and the other person doesn't want any part of it, don't take it as a personal affront but rather say, "All right, this is my treasure and *I* shall treasure it, and they have their treasure and I bless them to it." And remember, what you treasure may not be their treasure at all.

Participant: It isn't.

Gabriel: And you just allow them to find their own treasure and you keep yours.

Tinker tells me you have a new mode of transportation? Ah, so you go flying along now, eh? Well, flying low... Any others?

Participant: You told us that when we get into a situation that we want to understand the lesson or to get an answer for something, that we should center ourselves. I'm sure that I'm not alone in this but sometimes the answer gets to be a guessing game, "I wonder if it's this or I wonder if it's that," and it's not always very clear as to what the answer is.

Gabriel: Know you why?

Participant: Because I'm not centered?

Gabriel: You're not centered and also, even though you center yourself, if you go from being centered into, "Oh, I bet it's this. No, it couldn't be that. Maybe it's this other thing. No, I am not sure it's that either," and you start to speculate or anticipate what the answer should be, you block the answer from coming. But when you center yourself and you leave yourself open to receive, then is when you get the truth.

Participant: Okay, but I always have the difficulty of knowing whether I'm receiving the truth or my ego is talking to me about something. And I understand...you've told us in the past the difference between what the ego tells us and what the higher self tells us in terms of one being positive and one being negative.

Gabriel: Indeed. Your higher self always tells you that which is *constructive*. The ego will always insert fear.

Participant: I just have to be discerning?

Gabriel: Practice your discernment, beloved entity.

Participant: If you would please, describe for me the four states of the body once more?

Gabriel: Well, there is the physical, which is the molecular structure. There is the energy part of the body, which...the closest thing in physical form would be your nervous system. There is the mental aspect of your body, which is always under the obedience of the mind. The body has to do what the mind tells it to. And then there's the...what would be a good word?

Participant: The ethereal part?

Gabriel: There is the etheric body, yes. Now, are you referring to the mental body, emotional body, etheric body, and physical body?

Participant: Define etheric.

Gabriel: Oh, the etheric body is a very real thing. It's visible. The etheric body has all of the organs of the physical body, everything. It is an exact duplicate of it in a finer...it's the next step up from the physical. It is a finer...more gossamer in appearance. *It* only, of all of the bodies that connected to the physical body, it only disintegrates when the body dies. The etheric body will disintegrate at the same rate that the physical body disintegrates.

Participant: So you're not defining etheric as, or the ethers as, all of space that exists. When you say ethereal, that's the immediate dimension surrounding your ...

Gabriel: That's your scientific word, etheric, meaning non-physical but filling all space. No, the ethers are one step up in vibration from solid form. Now, there are degrees of it. The closest to the physical form... For example, the etheric body of the physical body you have...it stands out about that far [one inch] around in a blue-gray line all around your physical form.

Now, there are degrees of that. As it goes higher in vibration, more rapid in vibration, it becomes finer and finer and finer and finer and finer until it merges into the astral body. Now, that too becomes finer and finer until it merges into the mental body, and then the mental body, finer and finer until it merges into the spirit. So there are degrees of the ethers, just as there are degrees of the physical.

Participant: At what point does it meld back into the All?

Gabriel: I don't know if I can put it in your words because melting back into the All is rather a deceiving statement. Since the All is All-There-Is, it is never *not* in the All. But if you are referring to at what point does it cease to exist as an individual thing ...

Participant: Your separated consciousness, or your perception of separated consciousness, melding back into the All.

Gabriel: When you have... I still am not sure I have earth words to say it, but your individuality...you need a better language...your individuality becomes so vast and so all-encompassing that it melds back into All-That-Is.

Participant: But it's not actually a physical change. It's only a state of consciousness.

Gabriel: It's not physical. It's a state of consciousness, absolutely.

Participant: It's not even an ectoplasmic or any other descriptive form of any dimensional ...

Gabriel: No, no. It's far beyond that. It is the spirit absorbing back into the Divine Flame, as it were. It is the spirit...it is all of your essences coming up, being absorbed into the one above, to the one above, to the one above, to the one above, until into the spirit and unto the spirit it is absorbed back into what we would call the Divine Flame. I know not of any other way on your earth plane to use it.

But it is by degrees that this happens and it has absolutely nothing to do with physical matter at all. So, it isn't an absorption of the physical. It is the essence of your beingness. The physical body is merely a vehicle that you use while in the three-dimensional world.

Participant: Could this be likened to your vibration consistently becoming finer?

Gabriel: Absolutely. It is the same thing.

Participant: The crystals you talked about. They're up in the chambers, in the blocks. We're preventing them from coming down. Why would we leave them?

Gabriel: Because there is a tremendous amount of power in them and in the wrong hands or used in the wrong way, they could bring about a great deal of destruction, not just of physical form, but destruction...how can I put it?

Participant: Psychic destruction. Energy... destruction of energy grids.

Gabriel: It would be rather a destruction of the limitation around the energy units. It would be...it would not destroy the energy, for energy is indestructible. It merely changes form. It would simply go to a different form. But the barriers that contain... [Gabriel picks up a banana] This piece of fruit has a particular form, yet the molecular structure within it is filled with energy. Otherwise, it would not be a living thing.

Now, to change the form, one must raise the whole vibratory rate, the molecular structure of this living thing, into form*less*ness. When that formlessness is loosed, it has no form. It simply goes out and is absorbed into the All.

Now, there are certain rhythms to things, rhythms that bring things into form. The energy that is in this is probably the same energy that is in any other piece of...what is this again...fruit. However, it was drawn into *this* form. Now, to destroy the confines that make it into a banana ...

Participant: A more descriptive way to put it would be to de-atomize it. Is that what you're really trying to say? Or to change its energy, change it back into ...

Gabriel: Yes. However, the energy itself would not be destroyed by the crystal, but the form that would cause this to become a banana could be dissipated and there would be no form left to call this energy into the form of a banana.

She's telling me we have to close now.

Dear Father-Mother of us all,
Whose beingness is our beingness
and Whose love is our love,
I ask Thy blessing upon these, Thy children,
Thy issues of light and goodness
that Thou has brought forth.

Help them to recognize
the power within them.
Help them to know
the force of their own Spirit
and the truth that is in them
that they might live in peace with themselves
and in joy
and in the love that brought them forth.

And so it is.

Your Spirit & Your Soul
April 7, 1999

Rev. Penny Donovan: I just wanted to tell you quickly how Gabriel came to me and then I will leave and I'll let him take over.

I had been doing the Sunday service for over thirty-five years at Trinity Temple of the Holy Spirit in Albany and I went in to do the Sunday service and when I went in to put on my robes and things before I went up on the pulpit, I felt very strange. I felt kind of light-headed and I reasoned it away as being that I had eaten my dinner very early that day and perhaps my blood sugar had dropped some.

But when I got up to...the last thing I remember was the meditation, and then the next thing, I was standing behind the pulpit and everyone was on their feet applauding and I didn't know what had happened and so I just quickly sat down and I asked the chairperson, I said, "What's going on?" and they said, "Well, this wonderful entity..."—we didn't know who it was at that time—"...just came and spoke through you and gave us this wonderful lesson." And I got very nervous with that. I hadn't been told that this was

27

going to happen or anything and I didn't know what to do with it. I was very upset.

So anyway, the next day...my mother lived with me at the time. She has since passed into spirit. The next day I could hear her in the kitchen talking to someone—and we have a couple little dogs that are very barky and I knew no one had come in because the dogs didn't bark—and I went out into the kitchen and she's standing there looking up and I said, "Who are you talking to?" and she said, "Him." And I'm looking—you know, big psychic—I didn't see anybody. You know, I'm just...and she's quite enthralled.

Well anyway, finally I was aware of a beautiful light and from the beautiful light came a voice who said, "Greetings, Beloved Woman, I am Gabriel." And I said, "Gabriel as in *the* Gabriel or just somebody named Gabriel?" And he said, "No, *the* Gabriel" and I thought ... (Laughter) And I said, "Why are you here?" or I said, "What are you doing here?" and he said, "I've come to teach through you." "Mmm...I don't think so," and I said, "Why me?" and he said, "Why not you?" I said, "Well, I just don't know." And it took me about a year before I was comfortable with this because it seemed impossible to me that an archangel would come to me and do what he was doing, but he did. The funny thing...my mother always loved the Virgin Mary and when Gabriel said he was going to channel through me and I said, "I don't think so. I'm not comfortable with that," my mother slapped me and said, "Don't you talk to him like that!" Then she turned and said, "Tell me. How's Mary?" (laughter) like this was an ordinary thing. And he said Mary was well and she said, "Would you please tell her I send my love," and he said, "And indeed, she sends hers to you." And my mother accepted this, you know. After he left, I said, "I can't believe that happened." I said, "Gabriel," and she said, "Oh, sit down and eat your breakfast." It was like nothing.

And that was when he first began and he came every Sunday for probably almost a year that he came and he gave these lessons. And then he started doing all-day seminars and things like that. So that's how that began, and I wanted you to know that. Mostly, I wanted you to hear me because he is very different. And with that...I don't have any "going away" music so I guess I'll just...

Someone: You want me to hum? (Laughter)

Someone: Shall we sing *Halleluiah*?

Rev. Penny: Okay.

Archangel Gabriel: Thank you indeed! You are well this night?

All: Yes.

Gabriel: This is the first time I have come to your great metropolis [New York City]. (Laughter) Good to see your faces. Good to be here with you.

I want to address you this night concerning your Spirit and your soul, which is two different things. They are not the same. And in knowing about them, it is good because then you can *consciously* work *with* them because you are spiritual beings.

Are you desiring to come in, beloved woman? [Inaudible] Oh, you are all right out there? I don't want anyone to be outside the fold, you know.

The Spirit of you is that part of you which is made in the image and likeness of God. Know you how it tells you in your Scripture that God made man in His image and likeness. Now, God doesn't look anything like you because God is a powerful force, an individual holiness that dwells everywhere. Everything that you can look upon—your sky, your trees, your flowers, human life, animal life—that is all an expression of divine being, which is God. So God is limitless and boundless. He is all powerful. I will call Him "He." Actually It isn't a "He" or a "She." It is neither or both, however you care to look at it, but because most people think of God in the male gender, I will use that term.

Now, the Spirit of you is that aspect of what we term the Divine Flame—you call God, we call Divine Flame—because in Divine Flame, all things are. There is no separation from that aspect of holiness and life. Life in all its form is an expression of God, whether it be a flower, a blade of grass, a human being, it doesn't matter. It is all an expression of a divine force whose only desire is to become more and to express love, and the only lesson that you have come to earth to learn is love, unconditional love.

Now, that Spirit of you, that portion...oh, you brought me a bottle?! A jug? Well, we won't get into that. (Laughter) That part of you which is like unto God has all of the potential of God. You are creative. You are creators and human beings are the only ones who can create more than after their own species. Now, the birds that create more birds, animals beget more animals, people beget more people, but more than this, people create other things: this building in which you dwell; you fly through the air even though you were born without wings. You can do all of these things because your creative imagination has made it possible for you to envision and to know of things that you can bring into form.

So humankind...God gave to you free will and He said, "Go out and play and have a good time and create whatever you want to." And in that creation you have made your world, your personal world, and your experiences. You have created all of your experiences and you place them before you upon your path and you walk through them. And that all comes, that creative ability and power to do that, is the Spirit of you...is that aspect of you which is in the image and the likeness of God.

Now, the Spirit of you is boundless. It is eternal. You live forever. You *are* forever. The only thing that dies, as you call it, is your physical form. You lay it aside much as you would a worn garment that you no longer have any use for and the Spirit of you goes on eternally.

You choose any experience you want to and you create it in your thought patterns in your mind and then you bring it to pass. You put it upon the path and you say, "Oh, lo and behold, look what has come upon me," and you call it a disaster or a joyous experience depending upon what you have created, but nonetheless, you do this for the experience of it.

Now, a spirit who does not enter into the creative process is very much like a person who reads a book or goes to your moving picture places and watches a story played out. You're there, you're looking at it, and it's all very exciting but you're not living it. You're not experiencing it. You don't know what it's like to really *do* it.

But a spirit who comes and creates and comes to earth and goes through all the adventures that you create...you create some doozies, I tell you. You really do. But when you do that, it is different from those who just read a book. Then you are *in* it. You are experiencing it and from it you learn many, many things.

Now you might think, "Well, I have had this or that go wrong in my life. Why could I possibly...why would I choose that?" For the lesson that it gave you, the gift in it. Always, the gift is one thing: to learn to love unconditionally, to not love only that which loves you but rather to love broadly and all-encompassingly so that *your* life is a shining reflection of the love of God.

Now, because you create *so* many adventures, you go on and on, lifetime after lifetime. I don't know how many of you here believe in reincarnation. It doesn't matter. It is a fact. And you choose to come back to the earth over and over again. You never come back as a butterfly or as any kind of creature. You always, always come back as human beings.

And that's where your soul comes in because the soul of you is the *perfect memory* of everything that you have ever, ever experienced, every word you ever spoke. Your soul records everything you've ever thought, ever felt, ever experienced. However, the soul does not know the difference between truth and fiction or truth and error and if you believe a certain way, the soul records that belief, and it doesn't differentiate whether that belief be based upon fact or just your own imagination.

So...ah, we have a white blackboard, eh? [Referring to the marker] Can you take his hat off?

Now you understand, what I'm about to draw here is an *example* only. Your Spirit is vast. It is more vast than anything you could imagine. So here we have your vast spirit. [Draws]

Participant: S-P-I-R-I-T.

Gabriel: Angels don't write [inaudible]. (Laughter) Are you going to write for me?

Participant: Sure.

Gabriel: Oh, very good. All right. That saves me.

Now, the Spirit of you is vast enough to take in *everything*. In the Spirit of you, you know everything. That is a little hard for you to believe, isn't it, that you know everything? But you do and the way you know everything is because the Spirit of you is not limited in any way at all. Not at all in any way.

The Spirit of you has all knowledge in it and you get little pieces of it from time to time. Has it ever occurred to you how you know certain things that you never learned? But there are certain things that you just sort of know, don't you? And if someone were to say, "Where did you learn that?" you would have to say, "Well, I don't know. I just know it." That comes from the Spirit of you because in your Spirit you have all knowledge of everything that has ever been, what is now, and whatever shall be, you already know in your Spirit.

Now, that Spirit in you... Now, this little stick figure here, that's you. Now, from the Spirit of you there comes this information that comes down in through the top of your head, in through the crown chakra. Now, I don't want to get into the chakras tonight because it's a whole other lesson, but this information is ever available to you and all you have to do is ask to be made aware of a certain thing. Do your homework, get a background in it, and information will come to you. That's how *new* ideas are born.

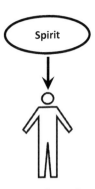

Know you how you have your discoveries? They discover this or they discover that. They discovered how to fly. They discovered how to get certain medicines to heal the sick and so forth. How do you think they did that? They did it through the information that is in the Spirit of you and when you ask, it is given to you. You must have a great desire, a loving desire, to bring forth that information and it will be given to you.

Have you ever noticed that sometimes when you had a great test to take, an examination to take, and you studied very hard and you went to bed very, very...and you thought, "I'm just so tired and tomorrow is that test and I don't know whether I shall ever get through it." Haven't you noticed how when you relax and you just take the attitude, "Well, I'm just going to do it. I'll do my best and I'm not going to worry about it," haven't you noticed how easily it flows and you get a higher grade than what you dreamed that you could? And you think, "I'm smarter than I thought." (Laughter) And it's because you've gotten out of your own way and you've allowed all of that information from the Spirit of you, which knows all things, to come in and to assist you.

Now, everybody does this. Even if they don't believe a word I'm saying, you still do it because it's a natural law, it's a spiritual law, and whether you understand it or whether you don't doesn't matter in the sense that you all use it always, all the time.

Now, the Spirit of you has a soul. Now, I know it appears to you that one is above the other. Actually, they interblend but I have no way of drawing that. So, this is soul.

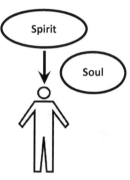

Now, soul of you has no mind of its own. It is a perfect, ever-working, never-failing recording mechanism that records everything you feel, everything you think, every experience you've ever had. And it records that which is true and it records with equal dedication that which is *not* true.

Now, when I say something is not true, what I'm talking about is a *misperception* you would have or a belief system that is not based upon truth. For example, if you believe that everybody in the world is evil, the soul records that and your belief system will be based upon that. If you believe that everyone is good and people do make mistakes but basically everybody is good, that is recorded in your soul and your life's pattern will be based upon that.

35

However, all of the experiences that you've had in all of your lifetimes are recorded in the soul and that information is equally available to you just the same as the truth in your Spirit. So that which is in your soul is equally available.

For example, let us suppose that in one of your lifetimes you were a great warrior. You went to battle and you fought and you slew people and you went forth in battle. You would have a subconscious knowledge of how to go to battle and how to fight and in the current lifetime, you would probably have an attitude of, "Don't tell me what to do because I'm going to do what I want," because you would have a kind of false fearlessness that came to you from your lifetime as a warrior.

Let us suppose that you went to the other extreme. Let us suppose that you were a great healer and you went about and you healed people and you helped people. When you come into a new lifetime, you would still have that memory and you would have an instinct to help people. Perhaps you decided to be a doctor or some other caregiver and you wondered why you always felt that was always what you wanted to do, because the influence from your soul would be so pronounced in your consciousness that it would kind of lead you into a similar thing.

How many of you here can play a musical instrument without having taken lessons of any sort? Anyone here play the piano with their ear? You do? Is that why you keep your hair short? (Laughter) You would wonder, "How did you know how to play the piano without having taken any lessons?" Because in another lifetime you played very well. Perhaps you were a concert pianist or something. But the point is that this knowledge that is in your soul from experience is available to you and it is part of who you are now. It is part of your belief system. It is part of your personality. It is part of why you think the way you think.

This is why some people have a very difficult time getting rid of a bad habit—or whether it's bad or good, getting rid of a habit—is because if it's something they've done in more than one lifetime, it's pretty deeply ingrained in the soul's memory and it's something that you instinctively do over and over. So, the soul contains *all* of your experiences.

Now, you have two sources of information then, do you not? You have the Spirit of you, which always brings you truth. Now, the Spirit of you is not influenced by the soul, not at all. The information from the soul, however, *is* influenced by the Spirit because the Spirit is the God of you, son of God of you. The Spirit is that in you which is all powerful.

Now, the soul is kind of like a great library in which all the information of your experiences have been stored and kept and are available to you. How many of you have found you start out in your youth and you think, "Well, when I grow up, I shall be thus-and-so"? And then when you grow up, you became something totally different. You go off in an altogether different path and you wonder, "Whatever happened to the idea that I was going to do thus-and-so?"

Now usually, when that happens, the first idea of, "When I grow up, I'm going to be thus-and-so," comes from the soul. That's a soul memory that's still influencing you. But the power of your Spirit is greater so the power of your Spirit would know that the *reason* you are coming to the earth plane is to do something different, something altogether different. So that information would come through into your mind and you would gradually change your thoughts and think, "No, I don't think I'll be this. I think I'll be that."

Now, the Spirit of you also influences your well-being. How many of you here consider yourself a positive thinker? You get up in the morning and you think, "Oh God, this is a good day." [A truck horn blows outside] Someone slaying something? (Laughter)

Someone: No, that's a horn, a truck horn.

Gabriel: Oh, is it a whole orchestra? (Laughter)

Someone: It's just a street noise. It's okay.

Gabriel: It doesn't matter to me.

The power of your Spirit overrides the thoughts and feelings of your soul. Now, when you are in your spiritual consciousness, that means when you have bypassed the soul and you are in line with the God Self of you, that is when new things, new ideas, new influences come into your life. It is from that aspect that you can *change* your life. If you're not happy with what you are or how you're living or whatever, it is from the Spirit of you that you make this change and I shall tell you how it happens.

The Spirit of you is ever in a state of grace. Everyone here know what a state of grace is? It's when you are pure, filled with love, loved unconditionally by God, and there is no consciousness of any wrongdoing in you. Now, that is your Spirit. Your Spirit is always in a state of grace.

In that state of grace, that is when you bring in the *power* that you have. Nobody knows how powerful they are. None of you know how...you all think you are victims of this or that or something else and in truth, you are ever in charge of your own life.

Now, you can be in charge of your own life in a helter-skelter, sometimes-I-can-and-sometimes-I-can't way, which is what most of you do, or you can *consciously choose* to be in charge of your life by using the highest, which is your Spirit Self, to think things through, to make your decisions, and to *live* from that absolute knowing, which is the God Self of you.

Well, you think, "Well, if I can do that, then why haven't I?" Because most people have in their soul a very strong belief system that tells you, you should suffer, you should be put upon, you are a victim, you can't win, and so on and so forth, and as a result of that, you accept what comes to you without thinking that you can make a difference when you *can* make a difference with a change of thought. Just a change of thought can make your life different. Now, that is a change of thought that must be held fast to. You can't think it today and not think it tomorrow or not think of it again for a week or two, but when you can tune in—and everybody can—tune in to that God Self of you, that is when miracles happen.

Now, a miracle is your natural state of being. When you're not having miracles in your life, you're out of your element, like teaching a fish to tap dance. But when you are in that Spiritual Self, what you would call a miracle is the natural out-picturing of your divine good. And where do you think that would come from? The God of you because God loves you.

Now people, in their soul, have these long-standing error perceptions that "You can't have this," or "You better not that." Fear. Now fear takes so many different faces. Fear very rarely stands up on its hind legs and says, "Boo." It is a *subtle* thing. It winds itself around in your thoughts and before you know it, you're making decisions based not upon the power of your Spirit but upon the error perceptions in your soul. You're thinking back, "I must have done this before and it didn't work because it doesn't feel right to me." You begin to doubt your ability, your right to have something, your right to be happy. How many of you here consider yourself to be absolutely happy all the time? All the time. Some days yes, some days no. Is that how most of you feel? Some days you are very happy and other days you are not terribly happy at all?

Your natural state is happiness. That's how God created you. He created you in such joy. If you could know how the heavens rang out with celebration when God breathed you forth because it was a great celebration indeed.

So there is this innate joy within you and one of the reasons people *aren't* happy is because they're not living... The joy that you have in you is innate. It's in your Spirit. Your Spirit is so joyous. That's all that it knows is absolute joy. It's great adventure for your Spirit to come down into form and to create all these wonderful little adventures that you go forth, but most people don't regard their life as an adventure. They regard it as a task, something difficult to get through, *hoping* that tomorrow is better than today, that kind of thing. But when you can feel the joy that's in your Spirit and express it...

How many of you feel that you are very spontaneous, that you can just laugh spontaneously, that you can enjoy life spontaneously? That's what you're supposed to do, you know, is be spontaneous. And how many of you feel you are this little person who must walk a straight line and if you fall off the line, you're in big trouble? (Laughter) Most people think that. Most people believe that they better watch out.

Now, some people believe that God will get you. (Laughter) Other people believe...oh, haven't you taught when you were a little one, "If you're not good, God's watching you. He's going to get you"? You've all been taught that. We shudder when that happens because God doesn't get you at all. God loves you just the way you are, absolutely the way you are, with no conditions attached.

But people have in their soul this belief system that tells them, "I better not. I better not." Has it not happened to you that when everything is going smoothly and you are very happy, all of a sudden you get afraid and you think, "Gosh, everything's going...something's got to go wrong"? (Laughter) And it does, doesn't it? Why? Because you believed it should. It should be wrong for you to be happy. It should be wrong for you to be prosperous.

Now, that's the other thing that people don't have a good idea of. They think of abundance as something

41

that has to do only with money. Abundance is a way of life. Abundance is the ability to take and to use and to experience the gifts of God, whatever form it takes, whether it be a whole basket of little gray kittens or a five-hundred-dollar inheritance or whatever. It doesn't matter. Abundance is God's way of expressing.

Have you ever noticed that God creates flowers in great abundance? And He doesn't say to a rose, "Well, I'm not too pleased with the color of you so I shall make a violet. That'll teach you." (Laughter) God doesn't do that. God loves violets and roses all the same and God loves people all the same.

Now here in your soul, in your memory, you have stored up negative belief systems based upon the past. For example, if in a particular lifetime you had a very, extremely difficult life—everything went wrong and you died young and all of that sort of thing—the next time you come back, you're going to have that fear hanging out there. You're going to be waiting for something to go wrong because it did before.

So here comes this information, this joy, this beautiful boundlessness from the Spirit of you. It taps you on the shoulder and says, "Hey, remember me? We were created in joy and your *natural state* is joy," and for a moment you think, "Oh, I wish that were true," and it doesn't occur to you that it *is* true. It *is* true.

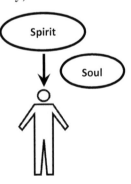

Now, one of the things that angels do is to help you with your thinking. They help you find the little jewels of truth from your Spirit, take them in as your reality, and live them and come to a state of joy.

How many of you feel you could be really happy if someone else in your life was different? Most people. Or you could be really, terribly happy if you had a different home and a different job or a different mode of transportation or something external were different, you could be *very* happy indeed. But it doesn't occur to you that the happiness you seek isn't *from* out *there* anyplace. It's from within and it comes from the Spirit of you through into your soul.

Know you...in your Scripture and I think in many scriptures the term, "Save your soul. To save your soul"? Know you what that really means? It means to cleanse your soul of negative memories, of misconceptions, of things that aren't your natural right and to allow there to be a *constant inflow* from the Spirit of you, which brings you joy and brings you prosperity and brings you good health and brings you all of the things that is your natural right to have.

You know, when God created you, He didn't create you and then think, "Well, that was a pretty good job. I like that. I like what I did. I wonder what would happen if they had appendicitis?" (Laughter) God didn't sit down and plan your illnesses, your sorrows. God didn't plan any of that. That was your creation and as you *believe* those things to be a part of your inheritance, you will create whatever circumstances you need to create to bring that experience about. How many times have you thought, "Well, if anything can go wrong, it will"? You do that, don't you? Wouldn't it be better to think, "Everything is going right and it will"?

I can tell you a little story of this Beloved Woman. She hasn't come much to your big city here and doesn't know any way of getting around and all that sort of thing. When she was invited here, she wanted to come, but it filled her with fear, "How will I ever find where I need to be?" She doesn't have much of a sense of direction either. Take her in the back yard, turn her around twice, and she doesn't know where she is. (Laughter)

So, all these months—because she's known she was coming here—all of these months, it has bothered her. She wanted to come but... "I want to go there but...," and it was always this same little nagging fear, "What if I get lost? I shall never be heard from again," and all of that sort of thing.

Now, she has a very lovely friend here who was born here, were you not? Close. So one day while she was sitting there beleaguering herself with, "How am I ever going to get through that city? How shall I ever find where I need to be? I don't know where to go to stay," and she's going all through all these things, we said to her, "Why don't you..."

Someone: Joyce.

Gabriel: I don't keep memories of names of you because every time you come back, you change them to something else so I don't bother. (Laughter) I said to her, "Why don't you call Joyce and ask her to go with you?" Oh, she said, "I can't bother her. She's a busy person." I waited a day or two and I said to her, "Why don't you call Joyce?" "I can't do that. She's a very busy person." So the third time I said to her, "Call Joyce!" (Laughter) I didn't say, "Why don't you?" I didn't give her a choice. I said, "Call her!" She did and this lovely lady said, "I would be *delighted* to go to the city with you. I should be very happy to."

Now, this is how the human mind runs. Here is opportunity. "Oh, wonderful, wonderful. Ooo, but between me and that opportunity, there is a pothole. There is a great ditch. Oh, there's a dark space and I don't know what's in that at all. (Laughter) Maybe I'd better not. Maybe that's not an opportunity." Now, haven't you all done this? You've all done it.

[Inaudible]...from up here in your Spirit. Now, you might think, "Well, if it's from her Spirit, why did she need Joyce?" Because God makes opportunities and the way to *use* the opportunity is created along with the opportunity. He doesn't give you an opportunity and then no way to do it. What would be the point of that? So when an opportunity comes to you, the way to do it also comes. And how do you tune in to that?

Well, she's not the only one in the room here with an angel, you know. Besides, I'm not her personal angel anyway. You all have angels and there's nothing that we like better than to be called upon. So, if you can't figure it out, all you have to do is say, "Angel, please help me to open from my Spirit the truth of this and how I shall do this," and straight away, instantly, they hurry about to do this very thing.

They took good care of you today, didn't they?

Participant: They certainly did.

Gabriel: Absolutely. Lots of little things could have gone wrong that didn't. And this is how it is, beloveds. God didn't put you down here upon the earth and then turn His back and walk away. In fact, one of the things He did when He brought you forth, breathed you forth into being, He said to us, "Look after them. They're going to need it." (Laughter) Oh, indeed, He did because He gave you free will. Now, we don't have free will but you have free will and you are creative and you can bring forth *whatever* you desire. It is how you *believe* and it is also how you tune in to the Spirit Self of you and *consciously use* the information that is there and the power that is in your Spirit.

It also requires you to pay attention to the voice of the ego of you. Now, I don't mean this in the Freudian—Freudian? Is that the term that you use?—in the Freudian sense. I'm talking about that little aspect of you that says, "You better not do that. Something will get you for sure if you go forth with that plan."

Now, the ego is fear. All of the fear that you have built up in your soul is the ammunition that the ego uses and it uses it to control you. The ego is your servant. Its purpose is to serve you, not to be your master. So, when this little voice says, "Fear. Be afraid of that. Be afraid of this. Be afraid of opportunity," then you can bypass that voice by listening to the voice of God, which is in your Spirit.

It's not hard. You might think, "Well, God doesn't talk to me." Oh, yes He does, every moment of the day. Every time you feel afraid, there is the comfort of God that says, "Don't be afraid. I love you." Who's going to fight God and win? No one, nothing.

So, God is more than any circumstance. He is more than any fear and it is your ability and your conscious choice to listen to the voice of God and not to listen to the voice of the ego. There are only two voices in your world. The voice of truth, which is God, and the voice of fear which is error. The voice of fear is never true, *never*, and it will never help you, ever. But the voice of God is always true and *always unerringly* helps you, blesses you, heals you, gives you courage, gives you strength. Whatever it is that you need at the moment, that is there waiting for you to accept it. And it's not that difficult.

Now, the soul of you doesn't store up all these error things to be against you. The soul, as I said before, has no mind of its own. It doesn't reason whether something is real or not real, nor does it reason whether something is good or bad. All it knows is that something is and if you have a belief system that teaches you fear, then the soul just hands it out to you because it has no judgment. It just allows you to be, to think, to have, and to express whatever it is you have within you that you want to express.

Have you any questions to ask of me so far?

Participant: You had mentioned that humans have free will but angels and [inaudible] don't have free will.

Gabriel: That's right. Humans do and angels don't.

Participant: I don't understand. I had always heard that is was the other way, that *all* beings have free will.

Gabriel: No. No, human beings are the only ones who were created with free will. Angels are created for a purpose. I am a teaching angel. St. Michael, as you call him, he is the warrior. He goes and does battle for you against your fear. We all have a purpose and we're happy in that. When I look at humanity and the mess you get yourselves into, I'm glad I don't have free will. (Laughter)

Participant: Can, as an angel, free will be a choice? Would it be...would that be something you have choice but not free will?

Gabriel: We have choice. We have choice. I guess I would differentiate it in this way. Choice is where something is presented to you this way and this way and you decide which way you want to go. Free will is a creative process. You create with your free will. Choices are decisions that you make, discernments that you use, but free will is a creative force. You can *will* something into beingness. You can desire it so ardently that you call in all the energies necessary to create it and bring it into form. So there would be that difference.

We are never allowed to interfere with free will of human beings. We cannot...even if you were creating a disaster for yourself, we can protect you, we can urge you, we can try to guide you away from it, but if you say, "Get out of my face. I'm doing this," then we have naught to do but to stand back and allow because we are not ever allowed to interfere with free will.

Participant: Because that would get in the way of the lesson that we're learning.

Gabriel: It would get in the way of the lessons and also it would take away your freedom. You are so free! Absolutely, unequivocally free, and if we got in there and meddled with that...

Have you ever met people who were do-gooders and meddled in other people's business, all in the name of doing good? (Laughter) And they get in your way and sometimes you think, "Why don't they just leave me alone?" But they're always there patting you along. They want to help, help, help. Well, we aren't allowed to do that although sometimes, I must admit, it would be fun, but we aren't allowed to do that and we don't. We know and we don't.

Participant: I understand what you're saying. I was thinking on one level but I understand you're going [inaudible].

Gabriel: Oh yes, free will is [inaudible] to us.

Participant: When you say free, when you talk about free, there are many people in these forms who don't have that type of freedom to do what they really want to do.

Gabriel: Because they believe they can't. They choose...

Participant: No, not because they believe but because of the circumstances where they are living. It's conscious where they don't have that freedom from [inaudible] of the people who live here in the United States. We are blessed by God and probably take everything for granted but people who live in other countries, but there they would like to have that freedom to talk, they would like to have the freedom...

Gabriel: Oh, we are aware of that.

Participant: They probably have the freedom to think but not to talk.

Gabriel: But if they chose, they could move somewhere where they did have freedom. The point...what I am saying... I'm not talking about earthly laws here. I'm not talking about people who are an oppressed people. You have always had oppressed people. You have always had oppressors. But you create...not consciously. No one ever sits down and says, "Well, I think I should be a victim today. I think I shall find me someone who's going to trounce the daylights out of me and take away everything I've got.

But before you come to the earth—when you are still in the spirit world before you come into form, the physical form—you get together with all of the people you are ever going to know in your life—relatives, friends, acquaintances, and so forth—and you all plan.

People come to the earth in groups. Some of them don't meet for many years on the earth, but they come together in groups who have chosen to experience a certain kind of adventure and they all choose the parts that they will play.

Now, I know this sounds very simplistic but it is the truth. When you get ready to come to the earth, you will choose your parents. Now, before they come to earth, they have agreed to be a parent to you. And you say, "Well, I killed you in the last lifetime. Do you want to kill me in this one?" "Sure, why not." (Laughter) And they choose to do these things and they play out that part always for the opportunity of learning to rise above it, to love anyway.

Now, I know that sounds difficult when you see little children who are starving to death and people who are so oppressed they have no hope, but they still chose that experience. Does that mean you shouldn't care about them or you shouldn't feel a love and a desire to help? Not at all. Not at all. It just means that *they* have chosen, for whatever reason, to go through that experience.

And the other thing you have to remember is the Law of Karma. What goes around, comes around. What you create will meet you. It will sneak up behind you and bite you in the backsides. So you think...the whole lesson is to think, to feel with love, because when you love someone, you don't create bad things for them, do you? You don't attack someone you love. So when people are learning love, then this wheel of karma changes.

Participant: Does this mean that humans can never be angels?

Gabriel: No, you're never angels. You go on and you evolve to great spiritual heights but you aren't an angel. We are a whole different species.

Participant: We can never become an angel.

Gabriel: No, but you can become a great and wondrous person. You already are a great and wondrous person. Everybody is but you don't become an angel. When you pass into spirit, you are in your spirit form, but you're not an angel. It would be like trying to make a little kitten into a rose. It's two different species. We're very different.

Participant: You said that reincarnation is a fact. I believe that. But can you tell me, is there an evolution? How do we...

Gabriel: Oh, yes.

Participant: So, in other words, in every life, we're a little more evolved?

Gabriel: Oh yes, you are. You never go backward. You never go backward. You always go up even if it's just a teensy bit. You always spiral upward, always. Life *evolves*. It doesn't go down. It goes upward, always.

Participant: And everyone can.

Gabriel: Everyone does.

Participant: I have two questions. Does the soul recording the karma represent...?

Gabriel: It holds the information from which you choose your karma, yes.

Participant: Would asking for spiritual help, would that be then like burning off the karma?

Gabriel: Oh indeed, yes. Every time you act out of love, even in your thinking...people don't know the power of their thoughts. Everyone here drive a mode of transportation at some time or another? Do you ever get from one destination to the other without getting angry at somebody? (Laughter) Frequently you don't. You have this happen or that and you think, "Look at that stupid...," and you get angry. Now, you might think, "Well, that's a harmless thing," but it isn't because that negative en...

All right, let me explain about energy. Energy is constantly moving. It's whole—everything about it—it's whole beingness, is *movement*, constantly moving.

Energy doesn't discern right from wrong. Energy simply is and can be *used* in any way, for good or for ill.

So, when you are having negative thoughts, you're pulling in energy that you're using in a negative way. That angry thought that you sent out to that other person in that other car, down the road is going to come back.

Participant: [Inaudible]

Gabriel: When you love. When someone does some dastardly thing and you think, "Well, I don't like what they did. That's not...I don't like it but I shall lift them in light and leave them in love and I know that they will learn better."

Now, that takes *you* up and it takes *them* up because there's no anger. You're not pulling in energy to use against them or against yourself. You're pulling in energy to bless, to heal. That's why watching your thoughts is so important. You create with your thoughts. You truly do.

Participant: If there's an evolution of lives, then how does one...is the end of that evolution [inaudible] to answer for the lessons? Is that predetermined as well?

Gabriel: It is predetermined by the individual. You might choose...you might look over and say, "Well, I've got this karma with this person, that karma with that person, this person owes me, I owe them, and so forth and so on. Why don't we do this all in one lifetime?" And you get together with them and they say, "Well all right, I'll do this and you do that," and so on and so forth and you get your karma all over with.

However, there is another way of dealing with karma and that is to recog...and this takes a...I don't want to say, "Takes a lot of effort." That's not true. It takes a lot of letting go, releasing, and allowing, and that is to recognize that you've never done anything you shouldn't and neither has anyone else. And there's *nothing* to be forgiven for.

Now, I know everyone in this room is thinking, "What!? That isn't true. I know this and this and this and that's terrible and that happened," and so forth and so on and you could all name me ten thousand things where you would say, "Well, *that* is wrong." But when you get into the *Spirit* of you, you recognize that everything below that is a result of your thinking and your creativity. You have participated in creating circumstances, even if it isn't a physical participation.

For example, upon your earth plane, now you have an area on your earth where there is a war, do you not? There's a battle going on. Not too many people are thinking kindly of the enemy. A lot of people are saying, "Go over there and *bomb* them out of existence." Now what kind of thing do you think that kind of thinking draws to you?

Life is supportive, it's nurturing, it's ongoing, it's ever becoming, and when you think thoughts that are destructive, you are going contrary to the flow of life and you are trying to turn everything upside down. And that's what war is. War is the *upside-downness* that is the result of people's thinking.

So any negative condition is upside-down thinking and to make it right, you simply forgive. Now, when you forgive, does that mean that you agree with what the person is doing or saying? Not at all. It simply means that you recognize that they are acting out of fear and not out of love and you are going to love them past that.

Now, there's a little verse that Beloved Woman is fond of and it goes something like...I don't know if I have it exactly. She's the poet, not me but it's:

He drew a circle of anger, a thing to flout.
And he drew it, that circle, to keep us out.
But love and I had a will to win
And we drew a circle that took him in.

(Laughter) And it's that same philosophy, to go beyond appearance, beyond what *looks* like has happened and into the truth, which is that life is good, it is lovely, and it is filled with all of the blessings you could possibly hold.

Participant: I have a question about cellular memory. If where we are reincarnated over and over and we have...we hold the memories, but yet we're born a newborn baby and we have these memories in our body that we lived in ancient Egypt or ...

Gabriel: Not so much in your body but in your soul. Now, the cellular memory comes from your ancestors—in other words, your parents' genes and their parents' genes and so on and so on and so on. That is what holds your *cellular* memory but the memory that is in your soul has nothing to do with the body.

55

Participant: But what about when many times when people do past life regressions and they have like a terrible fear of something around their neck and it's because they've been hung in a past life. Is that a cellular memory?

Gabriel: No, that is a memory that... You have to remember that your mind is master over your body. Your body will do exactly what the mind tells it to and if the mind says to it, "I'm being strangled," then the body, the throat, will constrict. And people have actually gone through—almost to the point where they passed away because they were remembering.

Participant: So past life patterns tell your present body where to hold tensions if something is unresolved?

Gabriel: Very much so.

Participant: So it's the soul's patterns of past lives that tell your present body perhaps where to hold tension or illness if its unresolved, at least.

Gabriel: The soul's influence. Very much so.

Participant: And that's the difference. And so cellular memory is your ancestral ...

Gabriel: Yes, it's what gives you the color of your hair and your eyes and any propensity you have for certain things depending on the race that you are or mixture of races that you are.

Participant: So the body is like a co-creation between memories of past lives and your genetic...

Gabriel: Yes, and what you want that body to do in this lifetime. Now, when you come back, when you determine that you wish to return to the earth plane in form, you carefully choose your parents, for lots of reasons, not the least of which is the kind of body they can produce for you to use. If you decided... Beloved woman, what is that game where they leap up and throw a ball through a circle? Basketball. If you want to play basketball, you're not going to come back four foot three, are you? You're going to come back in a tall body, are you not? And if you want to be a dancer, you're going to come back with a body that is light and graceful, are you not? So you choose carefully, very carefully, who your parents are.

***

Gabriel: You are refreshed?
All: Yes.
Gabriel: Someone came and asked me about angels and it occurs to me that perhaps a little explanation might be good concerning angels.

There are angels who work... There are angels above angels above angels above angels and so on so that we all have someone that we work *with*, and the angels who work *with* an archangel use that name and that is proper and right that they should do that. And when they do, a lot of people say, "Well, they channel this or they channel that," and they do to a degree but there are thousands of angels who use the name of Gabriel and there are thousands of angels who use the name of Michael and so on and so forth and that is all right. There's nothing wrong or different about that.

So, it isn't a *lesser* or *more* than, it simply is a difference in angels and that's all. It doesn't matter. You have angel help and really the name of the angel is very inconsequential. I gave my name because Beloved Woman refused to talk to a beam of light so I had to tell her something. You have a question?

Participant: Is there a relationship between animals and ourselves that lives on?
Gabriel: Oh yes, animals live on forever. They come back to the same person sometimes many times. If you have a beloved pet and you lose it or it passes into spirit, it will return to you.

Participant: [Inaudible]
Gabriel: She wants to know, what is the ego? Now, the ego...when you first came to earth, the ego had a very important part to play because... Don't forget, when you came to earth, you were fearless. You had no fear of anything. When you came to earth, you were very much still connected to the Spirit part of you, when you first took form, and because your life upon the earth was very short at that time—the average person going back into the saber-toothed tiger days only lived to be twenty, twenty-five years old, and then they were old and they passed away and so forth—and because you were fearless, you were constantly losing your bodies. You know, you didn't know not to walk off a cliff because where you came from, nothing could hurt you. So you decided you needed a mechanism to give you a little warning: don't walk off the cliff, there's a saber-toothed tiger behind the tree, and so on and so forth. So you created this...awareness, I guess would be a way to use it. You created this vibratory awareness that would tell you when there was something that you

needed to be mindful of. But it was never intended to make you afraid. It was only intended to assist you.

However, you all got lazy and you decided, "Well, I got the ego to take care of me. I don't have to think about that," and you gave more and more power over to the ego until after a bit, the ego—through use of fear, the fear vibration—through that use, became your master. And it was never meant to be. It was meant to be your servant.

Participant: [Inaudible]

Gabriel: Absolutely. It's only reality, it's only livingness, would be what you give it. However, the ego properly understood and properly used is a very good thing to have. It's a very good thing. It's part of your *instincts* as opposed to your intuition. Your intuition is the voice of God in you. Your instinct is that survival thing where you will survive.

Now don't forget, your bodies are very precious to you because, with exceptions of a few people who loan them out now and then, most people's body are the thing that is ultimately and only theirs. You can loan them your automobile or even loan them your husband but you're not going to ever loan them your body.

So, the body becomes very precious because it is so terribly *personal* to you. It's the one thing that is uniquely different from anything else in the world. No two bodies are exactly alike. Although you have all the same organs and blood systems and all of that sort of thing, you still are unique.

So, you guard your bodies. You have fear of losing your bodies and this is why you protect your bodies.

You take good care of your body—well, most of you take good care of your bodies—because you don't want to lose that because it is uniquely yours.

Participant: What are the lessons of the Holocaust and now with the conflict in the Balkans?

Gabriel: Because people are different, because they have creative abilities, everybody has their own idea of what a community or what any situation should be, but if all people acted out of love, there would be a harmony there. Even though there would be differences, they would not be antagonistic differences or warlike differences or conquering differences. There would be a blending. All the musical notes are different and that's what makes a symphony or a harmony, and it's the same way with humankind. Your thoughts are all new ideas, different ideas, and that's the way it should be.

The lesson of the Holocaust? First of all, we have to go all the way back to when mankind first came to earth and regarded his brother as enemy, and that began the hate cycle, which is based upon fear. What people don't understand, they fear. What they fear, they want to kill.

And so, when one regards their brother as an enemy, what they're really doing is fighting themselves because you project out what you *think* that person is like or what you *think* their intention would be and then you *attack* that. But what you're really attacking is your own feeling of guilt, of unworthiness.

So, when groups of people get together and they feel so totally unworthy, they create a situation in which they will be the victims of what they perceive to be a mightier person or persons. The lesson there would be love yourself, love yourself. Honor yourself, not in a sense that "Well, I'm better than so-and-so." Not that, but honoring and...you are a child of God. Think on that. A child of God. Is that not the most precious thing to know? And when you think that *everyone* is a child of God, there are no greater or lesser. You all were created equal. You all were created in unspeakable love and when you recognize that in each other and in yourself, then you're not going to see an enemy in your brother's face. And when people start looking with love, there will be no wars, no Holocaust, none of that. What would be its point? Who would there be to be the enemy?

Participant: So on a very large scale, it is fear that is driving people and they need to understand this themselves.

Gabriel: Absolutely. When you are afraid of something, do you not want to be rid of it? Well, it's the same principle.

Participant: How do you know what thought system to go with? The Catholic Church teaches that God created this body. The Course in Miracles teaches that God didn't create this body.

Gabriel: The Spirit...the Spirit of you is from God.

Questioner: So when we look at a baby being born, is it the body or the Spirit that is the miracle?

Gabriel: I would think that any birthing is a miracle. Whether God created the body specifically or whether the body is the result of the expression of the Spirit desiring to manifest in form, it is a miracle. All life becoming is a miracle, whether it is a flower with the buds opening or whether it be a woman birthing a child, it's all a miracle, all a miracle. And what was your original question?

Participant: How do you know [inaudible]...

Gabriel: What does your heart tell you? What *feels* to you like a truth? That's all you have to do is just what *feels* to you like a truth.

Participant: How do you start communication with angels?

Gabriel: Oh, just talk to them! You know, angels *love* to be talked to.

Participant: [Inaudible]

Gabriel: Oh, but you can. Now, don't misunderstand. When an angel speaks to you, it isn't an external voice. It's a voice in your head, so to speak. It's a knowingness within you. It's a feeling. It's a feeling. It's a guidance, an urging. Those are angel voices. Just talk to them like you would your best friend. They *love* to be talked to.

Participant: Do angels and spirits have a concept of time?

Gabriel: No, because there is no time. Time is an element of the three-dimensional world that humans created in order to keep track of things.

Participant: When we leave our body and we don't have a concept of time, can we go forward and backward in time?

Gabriel: Oh, yes. You can visit any of the historical time that you desire because it's all recorded in the Akashic records and it's all there exactly as you perceive it to be.

Participant: Is that why ninjas can be in so many places at the same time?

Gabriel: Oh, yes, yes. So can people in the spirit. You're all over the place.

Participant: And is that why God can be with everyone all the time?

Gabriel: All the time. All the time. No difference. No, you see... Time and space, as you call it, is particular to the three-dimensional world. In truth, your knowledge and your beingness is everywhere. You travel by thought. You want to be somewhere, you think it and you're there. You're limited here in the physical form because you've got these heavy bodies to carry about.

Participant: So if you are willing to let the body go, you can still do that?

Gabriel: Oh, absolutely you can. There are yogis and things upon your earth who simply put their body in some comfortable place and they go off and they travel anywhere they want to, and then they come back and pick it up later. They do do that.

Participant: I believe in miracles, but sometimes I get skeptical because miraculous things happen in my life and I know that they are blessings, but then they are taken away.

Gabriel: No, they're not taken away. They're simply changed to suit you better. And the other thing...miracles are your natural state but because you believe yourselves to be limited, you see a miracle— "Well, there's a miracle. We had a miracle"— when it's really the natural outpicturing of something that has always been.

For example, a person who is divinely healed— what you would call healed through the laying on of hands or through prayer—their natural state, *all* your natural states, is perfect health. So what a miracle is in that context is the person's ability to recognize that is the natural state and to allow that natural state to manifest in their body and they are healed. And miracles are never taken away.

Participant: [Inaudible]

Gabriel: Because people believe that's how it's going to be. I said early on you always think, "Oh, things are going so good. Something's got to go wrong." And so you pull that energy in to make something go wrong. And even though you don't *consciously* do it—you don't think, "Well, I'm going to make something go wrong"—you still bring in...that fear comes in, "Well, something must be going to go wrong," because you have created it that way. You have set yourself up to expect it to be wrong and so it is. But when you expect only good to come to you, good comes to you.

Participant: [Inaudible] Can you pray to an angel?

Gabriel: Oh, you don't pray to angels. You *talk* to them but you pray to God.

Participant: Should I pray to someone if I want to find my soul mate? (Laughter)

Gabriel: You want that...what is that...you have a song upon your earth, "Mr. Sandman, Send Me a Dream"? (Laughter) You want someone in your life to love? Well, be loving to those around you and you will draw that person to you.

Participant: I really think that that will happen.

Gabriel: Well, that's how it happens. You say to God, "I am tired of being by myself. I want there to be some loving person come into my life that I can love and who will love me and we shall be very happy together." And then expect that that to happen, but in the meantime, be loving to everyone. Be kind and gentle and sweet and you will draw to you that person. But if you're cranky and short with people and you don't like this one or you don't like that one, you're blocking that flow of love.

Participant: So, I just love everyone. I don't have to pray directly to an angel or anyone?

Gabriel: No, you can ask your angel to help you find someone. [To Tinkerbell] What? Tinker's concerned here. Do you know what I mean when I say, "Love everyone"? I don't mean to be promiscuous. I wasn't thinking...she's thinking that you might have thought that. (Laughter) I'm talking about being kind and gentle. When I say love everyone, *I* know what I mean. If there's any question, ask me because I don't want to mislead you into thinking I mean something else.

Participant: Are you saying that we should never be angry? Sometimes I get angry at others because of the lessons they are learning. As they are learning the lesson, they are attacking me. Don't I have to protect myself? It's like a survival anger. I don't think it's bad. I am just putting limits. It's like saying, "You are not going to throw this negative energy on me. I still love you, but I don't have to stay in your negativity."

Gabriel: When you set boundaries for someone—in other words, when you say, "No, I can't do that for you because I need some time for me. I love you but I'm not going to play that little game with you anymore"— that's different from being angry. All anger is always directed at yourself, even though you don't think it is. You always project out to somebody else what you're feeling within yourself against you. Nobody is ever angry with someone else. Everybody *thinks* they are but they are always angry with themselves and that anger is a misperceived feeling that somewhere, way back when, you did something God didn't like and you came away from God. In truth, you never left God, but people all believe, you all believe that you are separate from God and you're not, and in that separation there breeds fear and in the fear, anger.

Participant: When somebody attacks me, whether it's physical or emotional, I feel anger inside. Am I the only one that feels that?

Gabriel: No, you have a room full of people who are thinking, "I know what she's talking about."

Participant: I feel that that's okay. It's different for me than saying, "I hate that person and..." [inaudible].

Gabriel: But if, beloved woman, instead of getting angry, if you were to say, "I know that person thinks they are attacking me. They think that and it would *appear* that way, but in truth, that person is a child of God and I am a child of God and we both are loved by God and in that love, I love them. I don't like what they're doing but I love them and I know that their anger is going to dissipate. It cannot hurt me and I do not have to do anything except lift them in light and lift myself in light." And that is the only defense you need, the only defense you need.

I want to tell a story about a person who worked in a hospital and she was coming out very late at night and she had a ways to walk to get to her automobile. And she was aware that there were two men who stepped out of the shadows who were walking a bit behind her and she turned around and looked at them and she *knew* that they were coming after her. So she stood still and she surrounded herself in light and she *projected love*. She didn't say a word. She just stood there and she said to them mentally, "God loves you just as you are."

And they walked a few steps more toward her, then paused, looked at each other and turned and left and never went near her. It was because there was a force there of love that *completely* dissolved all their ill intent toward her because there is no greater power than the power of love. But if she had reacted in fear and had fled from them, they would have caught her and done terrible things to her. But she knew how to use the power of the Spirit, the power of God, and anyone can do that. Anyone.

So when you...the next time you feel attacked, just say, mentally say, "I know God loves this person." If you are feeling anger come up, you can say, "Father, right now I'm mad! But I need You to love them until I can love them," and you'll find your anger goes, because where love is, anger never comes to stay. They can't get along that well. Anger always leaves.

Participant: Are there new souls being born?

Gabriel: New souls? No, everyone was breathed forth at the same time. Well, people created their own souls at different times, you know, as they decided to come into form. Some people have never come to earth and they have different kinds of souls. Their soul is more filled with truth and light.

Participant: How can we learn to identify our angels?

Gabriel: You don't need to. Everybody has a couple of hundred angels with them. Oh, yes. And you just say, "Angel, please help me with this or that," or something and they do. Oh, how they love to be busy. They love to be busy.

Participant: The world is going through a lot of change. The problem I'm having is that there is so much chaos all around the world and it is starting to get to me. I didn't know what it was that I was watching on the TV program "60 Minutes," but I saw all of those dead bodies.

Gabriel: Why do you want to go there in your mind? Why do you want to tune in to that vibration?

Participant: Oh, I shut if off now. I believe in the light very much but I also really can't believe that they want to fight that way. I have a problem with that and I wonder where we are headed. [Inaudible]

Gabriel: Well, of course you would. Anybody would who doesn't realize the higher picture. Now, is that...does that make what they're doing right? Not at all. It's never right to slay someone.

Participant: But I can lift them up into the light but then the karma will be carried when their dead but what about nine thousand people a day walking around like that? Should we just forget them and leave them out?

Gabriel: You lift them in light and you allow them their experience. If you can help him, yes, but a lot of times people don't want to be rescued. They have chosen that experience and they want to see it through. And even though the rescuer in everyone says, "Oh, well let me help you," a lot of times the person doesn't want to be helped. They want to see it through to its conclusion.

You see, beloved woman, you have no way of knowing what that soul, what that Spirit, has chosen for its adventure. You have no way of knowing that. You can only see what's happening to them from *your* perspective.

Participant: You see little babies with their hands up to protect themselves. But if they had chosen to die that way, they wouldn't have shown the fear. They would have known.

Gabriel: Oh yes, they would have shown fear. But how do you know, beloved woman, that soul isn't paying back a karma? How do you know that in another lifetime they didn't do the beating?

Participant: So, why now? Why is everything so chaotic?

Gabriel: Because you are in a time of change, of evolution. The chaos that you perceive is the *old* putting up its final battle before it passes away. Negative conditions always fight for their life because they know the lifeline that they have is very, very delicate. They have to get people believing in evil. They have to get people believing in war and in killing and all that to keep itself alive, and more and more people are turning to spirituality.

Participant: How can we ignore the white light [inaudible]...

Gabriel: You just keep...you don't tune into the negative. You recognize the negative as an illusion. Does that mean it isn't happening? No. It means it isn't a truth. So, you *constantly* send *love* to those places. You send love to the perpetrators of those who would beat to death a little child. Now, you might say, "How could you love someone like that?" You don't love the *deed* they do. You lift them in love and light and you allow that love to so completely consume them that they are not *capable* of slaying a child or anyone.

Participant: I understand the concept. [Inaudible]

Gabriel: But God loves...just as much, God loves the evil-doer, not for their evil deeds but because they are His child.

Do you have children?

Participant: No, not at this time. I think in the past I've had them.

Gabriel: Do you have a husband? [Referring to the man next to her] Oh, you are the husband, eh? All right. Do you love this man?

Participant: Yes.

Gabriel: Has he ever displeased you in any way?

Participant: Sometimes he does. (Laughter)

Gabriel: When he is displeasing you, do you stop loving him?

Participant: No.

Gabriel: You don't like what he is *doing* but you love him anyway. Is that not so?

Participant: Yes, he's charming. He doesn't do anything bad!

Gabriel: He's charming and handsome and he's yours, right?

Participant: [Inaudible]

Gabriel: But that's your perception. But the point I was making, beloved woman, is that you are capable of loving someone who *doesn't* always make you happy. Now if you, as a human being, can do this, do you think God is even greater at it? So, God loves his children. Doesn't love what they do, but loves the child. And that's what He's asking of everyone in the world. You don't love the evil that is done but you love the evildoer because they are your brother.

Participant: But shouldn't people try to help the others? [Inaudible]

Gabriel: Oh, absolutely. You don't just say, "Oh well, that must be karma. Therefore, I won't help." No. You love them out of the karmic wheel.

Participant: At the moment of conception, is that when spirit comes in?

Gabriel: Spirit is...the moment of conception is caused by a spirit desiring to have a body from those particular parents. Now, the spirit does not occupy the little embryo until shortly before physical birth. They hover near it, they stay connected to it, but they don't move in and stay there because it would be very confining and very boring. But just before birth, sometimes several weeks, sometimes several minutes depending, they will come into the body and stay there.

Participant: In other words, the embryo does not require the spirit to be still alive?

Gabriel: Oh, no. Now, don't misunderstand me. It is *connected* to the embryo but it doesn't...

Participant: By the silver cord.

Gabriel: Yes. If this is the little embryo here [draws], and there is the spirit that wishes to come in, there is at the point of conception, there is a connection between. Now, this changes *only* if this spirit changes its mind and decides not to remain—doesn't want to take that body or doesn't want to come back at this time—then it will withdraw. Now, the choice here is if there is another spirit who says, "Well, if you're not going to use that body, I will," then *that* spirit connects and this one simply withdraws. Or perhaps, this one withdraws and no one else comes and then there is the death of the embryo.

Participant: Does the spirit consider abortion to be murder? [Inaudible]

Gabriel: Most...I have to be careful how I phrase this because I don't want you to think that abortion is correct because it's not. Any form of slaying, whether it be an unborn child or an old person—doesn't matter—is wrong because you are going contrary to the cycle of life, to produce and to bring forth. However, a lot of times a spirit will choose to manifest as an embryo for the benefit of the mother in order that she might have the experience of going through an abortion.

Now, a lot of people see nothing wrong in that and frequently those who don't see anything wrong in it will come back as an embryo who is going to be aborted so that they can know the fear and the acute disappointment, the rejection. So, a lot of times that happens.

All right. Now, let's get on with our lesson a bit more. How much more time have we here? A half an hour? Will somebody wiggle their finger at me when it's time to leave? I don't have time, you see. Now, I want to go back to the lesson here.

You can consciously use your Spirit and your soul to help you to live your life. And the way in which that happens is, as I said earlier, you can ask to be shown from the Spirit of you the *best* way for you to react or to respond to a situation.

For example, if you are confronted with a situation that you feel is going to be unhappy for you, you can say to your Spirit, "Did I choose to walk through this or shall I change it?" You always have the right to change your mind at any point, no matter what the situation is that's facing you. If you choose to *not* have that happen with you in it, you *can* choose to change your mind.

Now, how that would happen is either the situation would change completely and *un*involve you, or the situation would completely disappear, or you would be shown a way of going through it without it disturbing you. So there are many options open for you.

Now with your soul, when something is going on in your life and you're not certain how you should respond to that, you can say to your soul, "I want to know the positive, the loving, memories I have concerning a situation similar to this. I don't want any negative conditions in here." And you will be given a memory, not consciously. You won't say, "Oh, I remember this and that," but you will be given the feeling that will lead you through in a very different way.

Now you also have to remember, most people *think* they learn best through adversity. You have a saying upon your earth, "No pain, no gain," and that is not true. That is not true. You don't have to suffer to learn. You can learn in perfect happiness. You can. You don't have to be in pain to learn something.

How many of you here...I have to get help from Tinkerbell. How many people here saw the moving picture "The Lion King"? There is a scene in that in which the lion is beleaguering himself over trying to make a decision. He doesn't want to do this and he thinks he should have to do that and so on and so forth. And he's thinking it was his fault that his father was trampled to death and so on and so forth even though it wasn't. He's thinking that. So, the baboon comes up with a club and he whacks the lion over the head and the lion says, "Ow!" He said, "What was that?" He says, "What's the difference? It's past!" (Laughter)

Now, there is a very good lesson there. Don't hang onto past pain. Everybody has a horror story of something that happened in their life—their childhood, perhaps, or whatever—but it does you no good to *dwell* on it or to *use* it as a reason for you to be *less* than you could be now. There is no reason. It's over. It's done. Forgive whoever participated, forgive yourself for choosing it, and go on with your life because like the whack on the head, it's over. You don't have to think about it anymore.

A lot of people dwell in the past or they use the past as an excuse. "Well, I can't succeed because I was always taught that I was a failure." Well, who are you going to believe, the Spirit of God, which is in you, or somebody else telling you that you can't do something? Listen to the truth of you. Listen to the voice of intuition. That is the voice of God talking to you.

May I use you as an example? This little lady wanted to do a kind deed for this lady. What was it you were doing?

Participant: Getting coffee.

Gabriel: Oh, getting coffee, whatever that be. Anyway, she went out to get coffee and she thought, "I wonder how she likes coffee," and her intuition told her and she didn't listen. She thought, "That can't be right." So she came all the way back and asked her, "How do you want your coffee?" And she said exactly what your intuition said, didn't she? Now see, you could have saved yourself all that walking. (Laughter)

Now, this is true of intuition. *Listen* to it. It's that *gut* level feeling that gives you information when there is *nothing* out there to give you that same information. That is your intuition and *everybody* has it, not just the womenfolk. *Everybody's* got it. Listen to it. It will *never,* ever mislead you. It will never tell you an untruth. It will always take you where you need to be. Always.

Participant: How do you know the difference between intuition and fear?

Gabriel: Because fear says, "Oh, better watch out! Look out! Look out!" Intuition has no fear. Intuition speaks with love. The ego speaks with fear. With fear you always get an uneasy, an "Oh, I better watch out. I better watch out." With intuition... All right, how does this happen with a warning?

A good example is this: some years back, when Beloved Woman was a young girl, she had a long ways to walk to come home from her job and it was dark—it was dark early, it was wintertime—and as she got off the bus, a man she did not know—she lived in a small community where everyone knew each other—and this man she didn't know got off the bus with her and he paused to light a cigarette and she walked on and she knew he was following her. She knew it.

Now, she couldn't run away from him because it was too far for her to go. He could have easily overtaken her. So, she said, "Do I need to be afraid?" and this voice said to her, "No, you are safe," and she's looking about this remote area and she's hearing this man walking, walking behind her. And she thought, "Well, what if I am not?" And this voice said to her, "No, you are safe," and out of the bushes stepped a great large dog and the dog walked right beside her and she stroked him—an animal lover—she pet him and everything. The man saw the dog and he turned around and he left.

Now, the thing is, the dog was a manifestation of the protection. As she gets to the door of her home, she called to her mother to come and see this wonderful dog she had brought home and her mother comes to the door and she says, "Mom, look at this...," and the dog disappeared into thin air right before their eyes because the dog was a manifestation of the protection that she had. And he manifested, not for her sake, but for the man to see.

Now, when you are listening to fear...if she had said, "Oh no, I'm not safe. I'm not safe. No, no," that manifestation couldn't happen because her fear would have dissolved it. But she trusted. Now, you *have* to trust your intuition because it will *always* see you through. It will never, never lie to you.

Participant: I have been in situations where I felt, "I have to get out of here," and it was a good thing I did.
Gabriel: That's different. No, that's different. That is something that will take you...that's something to help you. That's the true work of the ego is to help you, but when the ego gets *unreasonable* and is causing you to

be fearful of things you really don't need to be fearful of, that is when you need to put the ego in its place.

Participant: [Inaudible]

Gabriel: Well, you simply bless it. You say, "Ego, I bless you. I love you. I thank you for the purpose in which you were created. Now get out of my face and do what you are supposed to do." (Laughter) It's that simple.

The ego...the ego is very obedient because it recognizes the only life it has is what you give it. And if you *really* get mad at it and don't want it anymore, it has no further existence. So it's not going to displease you, but it is going to try to keep you always needing it, needing it, and it's a false need. It's not a true need.

Participant: As we become more evolved and spiritual, does the ego become less?

Gabriel: The ego takes its proper place. I wouldn't say it becomes less. It becomes much less influential, yes. Very much less influential.

Participant: Does it ever disappear?

Gabriel: When you evolve high enough spiritually where you don't need it any longer, yes it does. It just drifts off.

Participant: Is the ego an energy form that is separate from us?

Gabriel: It's not separate. It's part of the whole of you, so to speak, but it operates very separately from you because its life depends upon you needing it, wanting it to be there, "Help me, help me."

Participant: Is it an energy?

Gabriel: It's an energy. It's an energy. It doesn't look like anything, particularly.

Participant: If I say it is not there, is it gone?

Gabriel: No, you can't say it's not there because it's an integral part of what you have created, but what you can do is to put it in its proper place and have it do what it was created to do rather than what it thinks it ought to do.

Participant: If we could see it, would it be a force, a spiritual force?

Gabriel: But you can't see it because it doesn't take a form. It is an energy that is influential but what does it look like? Nothing.

Participant: What do angels look like?

Gabriel: Angels are an energy field. We don't have a form. [Gabriel holds up a picture of an angel] You see this? That's a picture of an angel as people think angels look. We will always appear however you will recognize us so that you would..."Oh, there is an angel." But how do we really look? We are a beam of light, yes.

Now, angels borrow people from time to time to do a good deed. On the other hand, angels can manifest a physical form for short periods of time that looks very human, very real.

An experience Beloved Woman had on an aeroplane going from one destination to another—there was a stopover of some length of time—and there was a young woman there who had a child less than a year old, very active child, and this was a very small mother and this was a very robust, constantly moving little child. And the mother was very weary. You could see she was very of tired holding onto the child who was throwing itself and reaching for this and so on and so forth.

So while the aeroship sat on the ground, two young women came down the aisle and they started to admire this little child. And they sat on the seat across the aisle from her and they said, "Oh, may we sit here and play with her and hold her?" and they took her from the mother, sat right there in the mother's presence, and the one of the young women engaged the mother in conversation, "Where are you from?" and so forth. And the other held the child and bounced her about and all that sort of thing for about a half an hour and then gave her back and as they walked up the aisle, they simply disappeared.

And they were there to help this young mother with her child but if anyone had been watching... Well, several people saw it and they just melted away because all they needed those bodies for was that short little time just to do their good deed.

Participant: When we die, what happens to the ego?

Gabriel: The ego pretty much remains with the soul until you choose to return.

Participant: So, how do we experience death, physical death? [Inaudible]

Gabriel: No. Well, your death? You simply step out of your physical body like you'd step out of a garment. Death doesn't hurt any more than taking off a coat hurts. You shouldn't be afraid. There is nothing to fear.

Participant: [Inaudible]

Gabriel: Yes, and you shouldn't be afraid. There's nothing to fear.

Participant: [Inaudible]

Gabriel: Well, *all* of you understand. Only your physical body is the only thing that doesn't understand, but the whole—your mental body, your astral body, your Spirit, your soul—all of that is aware of the death process. Now, the ego stays around in the soul because you use the same soul over and over and over. You don't get a new soul every time you come to earth. What would we do with all of those old souls? So, that's why all of your memory is in the soul. All of your lifetimes is in that soul. And the ego hangs out with it.

Participant: [Inaudible] When I make my transition, can I go back to where I want to go?

Gabriel: You can go anywhere you please. Yes, absolutely. Once you're rid of your body, you just travel by your thought. In other words, you think you want to be somewhere and you're there instantly. Nobody says, "Well, your time is up. Back you go."

Participant: [Inaudible]

Gabriel: You can stay as long as you like, and you don't get a reservation either. You just go there. You just go there.

Participant: What happens when you dream?

Gabriel: When you dream? That's when you're traveling about in the astral plane. You create in the astral and those creations hang around you, and sometimes the dreams you have are things that are going to happen or sometimes you're just traveling back into something that used to be.

Now remember, when you enter back into the body to wake up, as you call it, sometimes in entering, the brain distorts what you have dreamed and you remember it differently than what it really was. But that's all dreams are.

Participant: While you are having the dream, do you realize you are in the dream, that it's really taking place?

Gabriel: Yes.

Participant: With chaos, [inaudible] changes.

Gabriel: Don't look at it.

Participant: No, I'm not looking at it, but where are we headed?

Gabriel: Something better. You're in evolution. The consciousness, spiritual consciousness of the people has never been greater than it is upon the earth now. You've come up out of a *lot* of things and you're evolving ever so slowly, but you are evolving into a state of unity and peace. You are.

Participant: [Inaudible]

Gabriel: What has computer got to do with your Spirit, beloved woman. Absolutely nothing. It's an invention that you are using temporarily.

Participant: I don't use it.

Gabriel: Well, whoever uses it. It's a temporary invention which is already becoming obsolete because they've already created something better. So don't buy computers...no, I don't care if you buy a computer. (Laughter) But the point is that those kinds of things have no meaning, absolutely no meaning, so you don't need to trouble yourself.

Participant: Can you change your dreams?
Gabriel: You can program to dream what you want to. You could say, "I would like to have a lovely dream about this or that or something," and then you will. But dreams are illusions. You don't get caught in your dreams because they're all illusions. They're there as long as you put energy in them and when you stop putting energy in them, they dissipate.

Participant: You said that the manifestation of illness is something that one wants to experience. How does one handle an ongoing illness such as cancer?
Gabriel: You just stop believing in it. First of all, as I said earlier, your body will give you *exactly* what you ask it to. Now, a lot of people find a great deal of benefit in being ill. They don't have to do something they don't like because they're not well or they don't have to take responsibility for themselves. Someone else *must* care for them because they can't. Sometimes it is a habit. People say, "Oh, poor me. Well, I've never been well and all my life I've *thoroughly* enjoyed ill health," and so on and so forth, so it depends upon the individual. But if you want to be healthy, then proclaim that you are, do healthy things, and believe that you are perfectly healthy because your body *has* to give you what your mind tells it to.
Participant: Is there a point at which you no longer have to learn that lesson?

Gabriel: A lot of people pass into spirit in perfect health. That's why they can't find what they died from. Because they didn't...they *chose* to leave at that point and did and there was nothing wrong with the physical body.

Participant: I meant if you had an illness.

Gabriel: You can stop it and reverse it? Absolutely, you can. Yes, you can.

Participant: What is meant by the phrase, "The meek shall inherit the earth"?

Gabriel: The meek shall inherit the earth? What are you going to do with it? First of all, you have to remember that all of your Scripture has been translated from Aramaic into Greek and then into French and into all these other languages and each language has its own idioms that describes a thing and the Aramaic language is a very picturesque language.

For example, where it says, "Jesus invited the young man to come with him and the young man said, 'Well, let me first go bury my father.'" Now, by that statement you would think the father was dead, wouldn't you? But what he was saying in effect was, "I would like to follow you but I work with my father. I help my father. Wait 'till my father is no longer here and then I'll come and follow you."

Now, "the meek shall inherit the earth," the meek represents that aspect of you of you which is...trying to think of an English word. It represents that aspect of the Spirit of you which is ever gentle and loving.

Now, to "inherit the earth" is quite misleading in those words because the earth represents a solidness of belief systems. In other words, your earth is solid. It has form. So to say the meek shall inherit the earth, meaning that the sweetness and the gentleness of the Spirit will produce a form like unto itself. In other words, your earth will become sweet and there will be no wars. It will be peaceful and harmonious.

It is nine o'clock and we turn into pumpkins, eh? (Laughter) I want to tell you that I have enjoyed being with you very much. I truly have and I shall say a prayer with you before I leave.

My Father God,
how thankful I am for these, Thy children,
with whom I could share
this evening of Your time.

I ask You to bless them
with love and light,
with joy.
Help them to live in joy, Father God,
and to recognize the prosperity
that is in them from You.

Bless them into the light of truth
and bless them into the love
that takes them ever homeward
now and always.

And so it is.

Good night.

Forgiveness
September 10, 1999

Archangel Gabriel: Tonight I desire to talk with you concerning your adventure upon the earth and to tell you why you are here. I know many times you have all wondered, "What am I doing here?" (Laughter) Well, tonight you shall find out.

First of all, remember, you chose to come here. Nobody made you. We are going to begin... Oh dear, I perished it. Is that all right?

Participant: It's good luck.

Gabriel: Well, it is not my desire to destroy.

[Gabriel draws] Now, this little pot here, we're going to make believe is your soul. Now, of course, you all know your soul does not look like a pot. (Laughter) However,  because the soul is the recording device of *everything* you have *ever, ever* thought, felt, said, experienced in any way, whether it be here upon your earth plane or in the heaven world or anywhere in-between. It doesn't make any difference. This little pot has it all in it.

Now, as I told you before, the soul does not differentiate between what is true and what is error. It simply records and *your* perception of what is happening to you and with you is recorded in your soul *according to your perception*, not according to anything else but according to *what you think*, what you feel, what you experience. That is what is put in this pot.

Now, mixed in with all of this in the pot is the element of truth of your being, the fact that God made you in His image and likeness, the fact that God loves you more than anything else ever that He created. Mixed in with all the stuff that you have created is this basic knowledge that *you are loved.*

Now, in your world... I want to clarify something. Your world is far more vast than the earth plane. The earth plane is only a minute part of your experience. You have experiences multifold in the spirit, on the astral plane, on the mental plane. All of these planes of existence are very, very real to you and very much a part of your internal experiences and very much a part of how you discern your life. So, when I say, "your world," I am not referring only to your earthly experiences for they are such a little part of your livingness, of your beingness.

Now, your soul records whatever is going on in your experience, whether it be on the earth in physical body or whether it be in the astral plane between lifetimes upon the earth, whether it be in the mental plane in your thought processes. It matters not. The soul gleans from your experiences and gathers it all up, much as a man harvests his fields and places it in its own receptacle, which I have depicted here as a pot.

Now, from the low astral downward into the earth plane, the ego is extremely active. From the high astral plane on upward, the ego's influence is very light and the higher you go, it becomes a nothing. But, because you are presently in physical form, because what matters to you at this present moment has to do with your physical life, we're going to address this night's lesson from the perspective of living upon the earth embodied in the flesh.

So, hanging about is the ego. [Gabriel draws] I'm a good friend of Rembrandt. (Laughter) This is the ego. Now, if you notice, the ego has a very diabolical smile upon its face. Sharp teeth...notice you that?

Now the ego, the whole criteria of the ego is to *prevent* you from knowing God. That is the only purpose that your ego *thinks* about or *dwells* upon or works toward is to keep you out of touch with your holiness, out of touch with your own divinity because once you have touched into that divinity on a conscious level and it becomes your reality, the ego knows its life is over. So, it works *very* hard and one of the ploys of the ego is to be very aware of what's going on in your soul's memory bank.

So, when you start consciously upon the spiritual path, which everyone in this room has done, when it becomes your goal to know God better, to have a better life and to live from your knowingness, from your spirituality, rather than from your fear... Now don't forget, the greatest weapon of the ego is fear. That is its sword. That is its shield. That is its whole intent...is to keep you frightened or out of balance, not confident, not trustful, not able to really, truly believe you are the son of God. So the ego uses fear in any way it can.

So, you are on the spiritual path... Beloved woman, you are higher than I am in her body. Would you write "Spirit" up here and draw two lines down as though like a funnel? Yes, indeed. Thank you.

Now, the Spirit of you—the God Self of you, that which is divine, that which is the part of you which is the son of God—that is constantly putting knowledge, knowingness, into the soul's memory bank. The Spirit of you is  ever feeding into your soul the truth of your being. This is what inspires you to seek a spiritual way, whether it be to join a religious organization or to read books or to learn to live better. It doesn't matter. It is all coming from the Spirit of you.

Now, as these ideas come down into the soul, they have an e...an e...what is it you call this? Eraser. They have an erasing effect and they go about in the soul and they take away false memory, anything that is not true. They change the vibration of it and they lift it up until the negativity of it is no more.

Now, the ego is not going to sit by and watch all this happen so here's what happens. Have you ever noticed that when you begin a spiritual journey, at first, everything goes well and you think, "At last I have found it. Yes, indeed," and then something *terrible* happens? Have you ever noticed that? You go along just so well and then boom, down you go. Now, what has happened? The ego has gone into the soul's memory bank and has pulled up whatever negativity it can that will stop you. It throws up a roadblock. It makes you think you can't go any further.

How many times have you gone along your spiritual path very nicely, then all of a sudden things happen? You don't get time to meditate or if you do meditate, your mind is here, there, all over. You can't seem to bring it into focus and the first thing you know, you don't meditate. You skip one, then you skip two, then after a while a week passes, and after a while a month passes and finally you begin to think, "When did I meditate last? I don't even recall," and it seems as though nothing allows you any peace.

Now, the ego has conjured up out of the pot a subconscious memory that tells you, "You can't do this. You can't do this." The aspect of you, the *truth* of you, the *beingness* of you, the reality of you is the Christ. And I care not whether you be Christian or not. Doesn't matter. You can call it something else if you want to. But that is the only Sonship...is the Christ, so all those who are the sons of God, which is every one, it is that Christ aspect in you that is the son of God and that is the truth of your being.

The only *voice* for God is the Holy Spirit. That is the only voice for God. Now, that is also the voice for the Christ. Jesus became the Christ through the Holy

Spirit and that is the path that you are on. You are doing the same thing. No, you don't have to be crucified and no Roman is going to come and get you. But you all you all are coming into, degree by degree, the awakened aspect of your consciousness that is beginning to *know* that you are the son of God. You are that Christ.

Now, there are only two voices that you ever have heard, that you ever *will* hear, that you hear now, that you...forever and ever and ever and ever, there are only two voices: the voice of the ego and the voice of the Holy Spirit. And those, beloveds, are the only two voices that you *ever*, ever hear.

Now, the voice of the ego is the voice of negativity, but it doesn't always present itself as a negative voice. It sometimes will present itself in a very reasoning way and causes you to think that you are truly listening to the voice of reason. Therefore, it should be a voice adhered to. It should be something you must pay attention to when all the time it is leading you further and further away from your own awareness as the son of God.

Now, why are you on the earth? And this is true of every single person on the earth with no exception... The earth is the place that you come to *to forgive yourself*. And that's the only reason anyone is here...is to forgive yourself. Now you might think, "Forgive myself for what? Be specific. What am I forgiving myself for and I will do it straight away." However, no one actually is conscious of what they need to be forgiven for, or what you *think* you need to be forgiven for.

Now, this idea of forgiveness is your *own* idea. It wasn't God's. He never thought it up. But because *you* think you walked away from God, you think God is really... [To Tinkerbell] What? I can't say. Oh, it 'tis? Is "pissed" a bad word? (Laughter) Oh! I hear it so frequently upon the earth, I didn't know that it was. (Laughter) I was going to say, "God is pissed off at you," but we can't put that in the book, can we? All right. Well, I apologize. I didn't know it was one of your swearing about words. Well, anyway, He isn't. He's not. (Laughter)

Participant: You can say, "Ticked off."

Gabriel: "Ticked off?" That is not a bad word? All right. Well anyway, whatever it 'tis, whichever word you care to use, He's not. But you think He is. Subconsciously, this is the cause of all your problems...is because this is what you truly believe is that God is really, really angry with you and somewhere, somehow, He is going to *get you*. Well, He's not.

However, the ego plays upon that idea with your pot in your soul here. So, every time a spiritual feeling, a spirituality, comes into your awareness, it bestirs the pot because it has to get *out* of that pot all of the negativity. So what happens? Up come problems that you had long since forgotten about—ideas, feelings, thoughts, belief systems—that you thought at one time were real such as, "My mother doesn't love me. She likes my brother better," or "I'm not a good boy at all. I'm really a bad boy. I know because my dad told me so." "I'll never get anywhere in the world because I was not born into money." "I'm really a lowdown form of life because I haven't got a proper education or because I was born on the wrong side of the tracks," or whatever or because you came from a dysfunctional family.

All of these things, *plus* the memories from other lifetimes which are stored in your pot here, all add to the idea that you are *not* the son of God, that you couldn't *possibly* be loved by God because look what a wretched creature you are.

Now, the ego knows that you will believe a negative thing quicker than you will believe a positive thing, and think about that. Think about that. You do. You will go quicker to a negative suggestion than you will to a positive one. Let us say you come up with a wonderful idea and you tell two different people. The first one says, "That's wonderful. I think that is grand. I cheer you on. Go for it." And then you go and tell another person and they say, "What do you want to do that for? You're going to lose your shirt. You shouldn't do that. I know someone who did that and they ended up in a terrible mess." Now which one...what happens there? You immediately become overly cautious. You immediately begin to *believe*...

Thank you, Tinker. What a wonderful idea. Know you how your financial institutions depend upon the people's faith in them? Do they not? Let a rumor get started that a particular financial institution is in trouble and its resources are very shaky. Now, it may not be a true rumor at all. It may be absolutely false in every way. But let that rumor get started and what happens? Everyone goes to that institution and takes out their funds, do they not? As they take out their funds, what happens to the institution? It comes true. The institution fails because everyone has gone and withdrawn their funds from it.

Now, this happens in people's lives in things that...where the ego uses the ploy of something negative is going to happen to you. If you do thus-and-so or if this or that happens, you're in for a bad time.

Now, back to the two voices. The voice of the ego is the one who's saying, "You better not do that," or "This is not for you. Why are you doing this?" or worse yet, "You're going to have bad health. Your finances are very shaky. You'd better not," or "You know, your mate has been acting strange of late. If I were you, I'd keep an *eye*..." or some such thing. Or "Are you sure that person is really your friend? They made the most peculiar remark the other day. Are you sure they can keep a secret?" All these little...that is the voice of the ego.

Now, the voice of the Holy Spirit is a soft and gentle voice. It never shouts above the ego's voice but it will come in with comforting words. It will tell you things like, "You look so pretty today," or "You were so wise in what you just did," or "God really loves you. Did you notice the sunset that He placed there for your pleasure?"

The Holy Spirit sees you as the son of God. The Holy Spirit also sees all of the illusion that you create around yourselves that you believe in that is not true, such as: you can't succeed; you can't be healthy; you can't have a secure home; you can't do this; you can't do that.

Now, each time this pot gets stirred up, the ego rushes in and it grabs every negative thing it can find and it brings it right up and it casts it upon your path.

Beloved woman, may I use you as an example? This beloved soul has had many things go wrong in her life the past few weeks, have you not?

Participant: Oh, yes.

Gabriel: Automobiles that won't run, husbands that won't run. (Laughter) Or perhaps, Tinker says, "No, they run too much," the husband. Whatever. Anyway, one thing upon the other. Now, I can tell you why, with her, and the same thing applies to every one of you when things like that happen. She is on a spiritual path, *very* dedicated to her spiritual path, and she is growing by leaps and bounds on her spiritual path and she is coming to a time when she must have absolute *freedom* from all limitation.

Now, how can that happen when her automobile won't run and her husband must be cared for twenty-four hours a day and things are going wrong with her home—this needs fixing, that broke down, the other thing isn't working right, and all of this? Now, how can she be free to pursue her spiritual path when everything in the earth plane is calling her name and pulling at her and saying, "You've to take care of me. You've got to take care of me. You must pay attention here. You have to do this. You have to do that," until this dear lady is fragmented to the point where she doesn't know whether she's the Christ or not. Is that not so?

Participant: Yes, today was...

Gabriel: Today was one of those days. Now, I can tell you, you've all had times like this, every one of you. Different circumstances but you still have all had times like this and here is why. The ego will put upon your path *anything* out of your *pot* that it can cast upon your path because it knows you will believe in it. Why? Because it comes out of your *own very soul.* It is *yours.* It is *not* anyone else's. It is *yours* so the ego has a very workable weapon here. You're going to believe it. Why? Because it happened before. It's familiar territory. You *know* about this because you've been there and done that.

So, now here come the two voices. There is the voice of the ego saying, "See, I told you you can't be on a spiritual path. Look at all of the responsibilities you've got." Is that not so? Now, you can believe that and you can fall into that trap, which...what does that do? That adds to the belief that God doesn't love you. What could make you feel more unloved than to have everything in your life go wrong? You think, "What? I'm chopped liver?" (Laughter) You aren't going to believe the love and comfort of God because everything is such a mess in your life.

So, is there any way to make you feel more abandoned, more unworthy, than to have everything in your life go wrong? Not at all, and the ego sits back with its little satisfied look and says, "Ha, did it again. Damn, I'm good."

Now, what does one do with that? You tune out the voice of the ego and you listen for the soft sweetness of the voice of the Holy Spirit. The Holy Spirit will say to you, "This is an illusion that you created and as you have created it, you can *un*create it. As you have made it your truth, you can *un*make it your truth."

Now, how does one do that? One does that by the very reason you are here and that is to *forgive yourself*. Since most people have a very misperception of what they need to be forgiven for, it doesn't do a whole lot of good to sit and think about your so-called sins because usually none of them make any difference anyway. It doesn't matter. It's all an illusion. It's something that was created by you to walk through and has absolutely no value whatsoever, so you have to trust the Holy Spirit to take you *past that* because that is only an erroneous belief system.

In order for you to forgive yourself, you *have to* forgive everyone else because that is the only way to self-forgiveness. It is the only road that self-forgiveness has...is to forgive *everyone* that you perceive has ever done anything *to* you that *you* think was a wrong. The truth be that they didn't do anything, but while you are in that belief system that they did, the only way is to forgive them.

Now, most people will sit and think, "Well, I've forgiven everyone. I don't hold any grudges. Not a one." How are things in your life? "Awful. Oh, couldn't be worse." But you don't hold anything against anyone? "Oh no. No." If you don't hold anything against anyone, why is your life a mess? "Beats me. These people keep *doing* things."

Now, if you believe that someone is *doing* things, then you have not forgiven anyone because those who have truly forgiven know the peace of God. Because when you have no ill will, no memory that you cling to and treasure of some misdeeds done against you, in rushes the peace of God and the peace of God opens the door to your realization that you are loved by God deeply, profoundly, eternally, and that nothing in your life has any meaning excepting that *you are loved* and you are forgiven. And those things will set you free of *all* of the other stuff that you cling to, that you hold fast to. That is why you are upon the earth.

God has His methods of teaching you. First of all, He gave the Holy Spirit complete power to do with the individual whatever it needs to do to bring you up into your awareness of the son of God.

Have you ever wondered why certain people come into your life at certain times? Have you ever wondered where, out of the blue almost, it seems a person will come who proves to be a dear and treasured friend? Equally so, out of the blue, comes a person who appears to be the devil incarnate. Have you not noticed that?

Now, that's God's plan, you know. That's God's plan. There is a reason for both of these people in your life. The dear friend is there to bolster you up, to give you strength, to support you, to make you know how much you are loved. Now the devil incarnate, on the other hand, is there...that is the one to treasure. The enemy is the one you treasure because therein lies the lesson. The friend is there for an arm around the shoulder, a pat on the back, a hug, a phone call. "Are you all right? I want you to know I love you."

But the *enemy*...there is the work of God afoot because how are you going to learn forgiveness if there be none to present themselves to you to be forgiven? How do you learn to swim if you don't get in the water? You don't. You don't put on a pair of skis to go swimming, do you? [To Tinkerbell] Well, oh not those kinds. I'm talking about the ones in snow. (Laughter) I should have used another...yes, all right. You don't climb upon a horse to learn to swim, do you? No, indeed. [To Tinkerbell] Now do something with that! (Laughter) Not a seahorse! No, not a seahorse. (Laughter) She's so smart!

The one who teaches you the most is frequently the one who presents themselves in your life as the most *trying* person you have ever met. The one who offers you the biggest opportunity to *forgive* is the one who does *everything you hate*. The one who riles you up, who makes you angry, who makes you think, "Oh, I give up. I can't. It's no use." The one who pushes all your buttons is the one that is your dearest ally because that person is giving you an opportunity to come up out of the ego's belief system and into the *knowingness* of the Christ who says, "There's nothing you can say or do to me that's going to hurt me because the son of God cannot be hurt, the son of God cannot be attacked, and the son of God cannot be injured in any way or form whatsoever. So therefore, I bless you, dear friend. In all of your antagonistic ways, I bless you and I thank God for you and I forgive you and I release you and I let you go to your highest good and I thank you so much for the opportunity that you have afforded me to *forgive you with love*." *That* is why you're all here.

Now, forgiving...every time you forgive someone, whether it be for a *little* thing or a *huge* thing—makes no difference—there is no difference in the value of what you are forgiving for. A little forgiveness has as much value as a great forgiveness. It is the act of forgiveness that forgives you, for forgiveness is a strange thing. Whenever it is given, it comes back to embrace the giver. Whenever it is given, it comes back to free the giver. It isn't the person being forgiven that is getting the value of this. It is the person *doing* the forgiving that is getting the value of it and that is very important.

Now, forgiveness is only...I shouldn't say only. Not only. Forgiveness is the foundation, the deep, abiding, eternal foundation upon which is built the Sonship of God, which includes all people, because it is in forgiveness that you come to recognize after a bit, as you forgive and as you grow and as you forgive and you grow, you come to the point where you recognize there is nothing to forgive and there never has been. And when you come to that, guess what? You have forgiven yourself. You have forgiven yourself.

I want you to take a little break...[inaudible]... about what I have just said about forgiveness. I want you to really bring it into your awareness as to what the meaning of my words have for you. When we come back, we will continue but I don't want to continue until I know you have it truly within you what I have just said, because otherwise the rest of tonight's lesson is going to seem too difficult.

***

Gabriel: Did you give careful thought to what I said about forgiveness?

All: Yes.

Gabriel: Misperception...no, let me change that. Perception can be very misleading because perception is based only upon your idea of what is happening to you. Two people can have the very same experience and each one will have a different version of what is going on. One of them will say, "Oh, I thought it was wondrous indeed," and the other will say, "It was absolutely awful."

Now, every time you forgive someone... First of all, let me explain... When you forgive someone, that does not mean you condone their actions or their words, as the case may be. That doesn't mean you say, "Oh, it's all right that you run over me with your automobile. I don't mind the tire marks up my back at all!" (Laughter) Hs nothing to do with that. What it does have to do with is your realization that no one can do anything to you that you have not invited them to do.

Now you might think, "I would *never* have invited that so-and-so to do what he did." On another level you have. Now, here is what you must understand. Every single person in your life, whether it be a relative, friend, acquaintance, neighbor, employer, employee—doesn't matter—every single person in your life is there *because you invited them*, just as *they* invited you into *their* experience. It's a two-way street, you know. And you are doing to them, whether it be good or ill—it doesn't matter—you are doing to them exactly what they invited you to do for the purpose of the experience of forgiving.

Now, why is forgiveness so important? Because it is your only way home. It is your only way back to where you know you are loved by God, to where you know you are the Christ. Not the only Christ. It isn't a thing where you're going to think, "I'm the Christ and nobody else is. Got it made. Me and old J.C. We're just like that!" No, not that.

The Christ is a state of consciousness which the man Jesus attained to. He got to be there and this is what everyone else is in their journey doing also...is getting to be in that state of *awareness*. So, Christhood is a state of awareness that a man named Jesus who lived two thousand years ago got into. He attained that awareness.

Now, he did that for himself but in doing it for himself, he also opened the way for everyone else because, as he told you, "What I have done, you can do also." He tells you that. Now, everyone thinks that means you're going to go about doing miracles. You're going to make the blind to see and the halt to walk and you're going to walk on water and if you're playing golf and the ball goes in the water, you're going to put your hand and it's going to come to the surface. You're going to walk out on the water and smack that little sucker into kingdom come! (Laughter) No, not that.

Being aware in the Christ consciousness simply means that you see God in everyone, as well as in yourself, that you are *aware* that everyone who comes into your life is a potential Christ, just as *you* are a potential Christ.

Now, forgiveness takes you to that. [Gabriel draws] Let us say that this is the potential...oh, I have one that is of a different color, another race! (Laughter) I didn't know they made them in different races. They do. Isn't that wondrous indeed. (Laughter) Well, this little one here...oh, that's not the right letter. I'm looking to spell "Christ." Come and spell "Christ." Tinker says that's wrong. What's wrong with it? Well, finish it while you're there.

Now, the Christ is already...the Christ awareness is already within you but you have covered it over with all of the guck that you have believed in through the years. So, what happens as you forgive, as you truly, truly forgive. You remove a layer that obscures the Christ and that Christ rises higher in your consciousness.

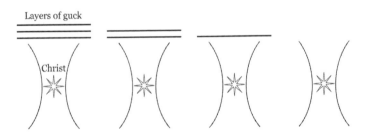

Then the next time you forgive, another layer is removed and the Christ awareness rises a little higher until at last you have nothing to obscure your view and your awareness of your own Christ, and not yours only, but of the Christ that lies within everyone.

Everyone in this room has someone that they need to look at differently, someone they need to view, not as an obstacle on the path of their unfoldment but rather as an opportunity on their path to love unconditionally, and that is accomplished through forgiveness.

Now, does that mean that you will always like everything this person does or says? No, but you will recognize that when they are doing or saying something that goes against your grain, as your term is, that it is not done out of maliciousness. It is not done to hurt you. It is done in order that you have yet another opportunity to forgive. And you might think, "Well, how many times have I got to forgive this bozo?" (Laughter) Until you recognize that that bozo is not the problem.

Now, where do you think you would find the Christ? Within. Where do you think you find your bozos? (Laughter)

Participant: Outside. (Laughter)

Gabriel: No. You of all people should know better! (Laughter) You find your bozos within, too. Now, here's how it works.

When you have a need to rise up in forgiveness, you will find someone presenting themselves to you upon whom you can project your own problem. In other words, you can find someone else to *blame* for you feeling badly. Everyone familiar with that? So, when that happens, what do you suppose is actually, truly going on?

Participant: It is a reflection of what is going on inside of you.

Gabriel: It is indeed a reflection of what is going on inside of you. Whenever you see someone that *you* *think* is an enemy, regardless of in what term you care to apply that, whether it be someone who is robbing you of your happiness or taking away love or whatever, the truth be that you have within you the very thing that you are despising within them. Now, you might say, "Well, *I'm* not capable of killing." Well...or "I don't steal. I would never do that." You have that consciousness in you. I didn't say you would act on it. Most people have a lot of anger inside of them that they never act on but does that mean it isn't there? Not at all.

Now, while you hold that anger in you, there is going to come triggering mechanisms to bring it forth, even if it's in little pieces, even if you get mad at your neighbor because his dog comes over and destroys your garden. It doesn't matter what or who you are angry at. You can know that the anger you are projecting out to that individual is within you. And who are you angry at? Them? Not at all. You're angry at yourself and, the big one is, you're really angry at God.

Now, most people find it unacceptable to be angry with God. "Oh, I wouldn't dare be angry with God. Ooo." That's quite true. Tinker says, "With exceptions of this Beloved Woman who doesn't mind calling Him out on things." (Laughter) But anyway, she'll get over it. The thing is that the anger that you *think* you have toward God and toward yourself is really your unwillingness to accept the love that is already within you. How many of you, and let this be an honest answer, can truly say you deeply love yourself? Oh my, look at all those hands. (Laughter) Not a one of you.

[To a participant] You think you deeply love yourself? Did you deeply love yourself a few years ago when you beat the daylights out of your body in an automobile accident?

Participant: I guess not. (Laughter)

Gabriel: I guess not, indeed. Not to tell tales out of school on you. I don't mean it that way. But you will do to yourself nasty things. You will do to yourself nasty things because you have this anger in you.

Now, what is the *root* of your anger? *You* think you walked away from God. You walked away from a *good thing* and now you're kicking your own backsides down through eternity for doing it. But the truth is, beloveds, you *didn't* walk away. You *didn't* do any of the things you think you did. Now, forgiveness is the way to coming to recognize that you truly never did anything wrong.

Now, you project blame onto others. This is why we teach you to *forgive* others because as long as you can blame them, then *they* have to be the object of your forgiveness too. Because as you would blame, you forgive. As you forgive, you come up in consciousness. You find you blame a little less. You forgive more. You overlook more. You are willing to be patient and tolerant of someone. Most people are far more tolerant of others than they are of themselves. So you see, the whole adventure here upon the earth is for you to have the opportunity to *forgive yourself.*

Oh, that's a good thought. Tinker had an idea. [To a participant] Beloved entity, you teach forgiveness. What do you find people have the greatest obstacle doing?

Participant: I think the first part is making that transition in thinking that you spoke about, to understand that the problem is not outside. The problem is within. The problem is how I am viewing the situation. I think that's the first obstacle. The second part is really accepting the forgiveness of oneself. Accepting the love of oneself is the hardest thing.

Gabriel: Indeed. And how are you doing with those two things?

Participant: Very good. Very, very good! (Laughter) A lot better than before. I'm very proud of myself.

Gabriel: Oh, yes. Indeed, you should be. And you did it right by the seat of your pants, quite literally.

Participant: Thank you. Yes, I did. (Laughter) I was in one of those pissed off moods, you know? (Laughter) I feel great.

Gabriel: Ah, yes indeed. But have you not noticed, beloved entity, that you are less angered?

Participant: Yeah, I seem to be laughing more, a lot more.

Gabriel: And why do you think that is so?

Participant: Because my way was hopeless and going nowhere fast. (Laughter)

Gabriel: And when you turned it over to the Holy Spirit, things turned around, didn't they?

Participant: Oh, yeah, yeah. I was so willing to do that. (Laughter)

Gabriel: He wasn't willing at all to do it. Every time it was presented to him, he got out his sword and he said, "Don't you come near me, you Holy Spirit." (Laughter)

Participant: This is true.

Gabriel: Yes, indeed. We know. Tinker used to come fleeing to me. She'd say, "Do you know what he said now?" (Laughter) Oh, we heard all about it. Thank you, beloved.

The point is, beloveds, that you very rarely see for yourselves that the problem as the answer lies within you, and when you consistently look out there for someone else to make it better by doing something or getting out of your life or whatever it is you expect is going to happen, you have to stop and ask yourself, "What do they represent to me? What is their presence in my life symbolic of within me? What is their action or the words or whatever the problem might be—what is that within me?"

Tinker is bringing to my mind some good thoughts here concerning... She said, "People don't always express it in anger. Sometimes they express it in depression." Anyone here have problems with depression from time to time? I think everybody does.

Anger is a strange thing. It wears many faces and one of those faces is depression. And depression is also a strange thing. It's a very subtle thing. People usually get well into it before they recognize it. It's one of those things that sort of creeps upon you and doesn't even let you know it's there until it has its roots deeply embedded in your psyche, and then you become aware that you are depressed.

One of the symptoms of depression is a lack of caring. "I don't care. If you want to do that, you go right ahead. I don't care. I don't care." The other is an abiding sorrow that seems to have no basis, a sadness that doesn't ever seem to get better, a feeling of deep grief without there being an external purpose behind it.

That is anger, unexpressed as anger, but nonetheless it is anger and its roots lie in the realization that you have to be forgiven. It doesn't matter if you don't know what for. Most people have not a clue. You don't actually have to be forgiven for anything but because you believe you do, that is your awareness. And even though you don't think, "I was a terrible person, so therefore God must forgive me," you may not even consciously have any connection with that, but underneath in the *pot* of your soul, there is the belief that somewhere, sometime, you did the unforgivable.

Now, because it isn't necessary for you to *know* it, all that is necessary is for you to be aware of that feeling is here in the soul. Now is when you listen to the voice of the Holy Spirit and you ask the Holy Spirit to come in and to intervene in your life and to take from you that which you do not see.

Now, that takes many steps. It isn't a single step. Now, the Holy Spirit comes instantly. The moment it is invited, it is there. But most people go through a *series*. They ask the Holy Spirit to come and for a little while things get better. Then things get worse again because, as I said, the ego will call up things.

But the other reason things get not so good anymore is because you take back from the Holy Spirit that which you have given. You say, "Come and help me," and then you say, "No, don't help me." Now, you don't consciously say, "No, don't help me." Sometimes you are working outwardly very hard at being helped, but inwardly you are not releasing to the Holy Spirit's power the grief, the anger that you are holding on to and so it will reoccur. When it reoccurs, simply ask again. Choose *again* to have the Holy Spirit come and take it from you.

Now, you may have to do this many times over because everyone treasures their fears and their anxieties. Everyone treasures them even though they say, "Oh, I wish someone would come and take this away from me." If someone did, they would say, "Get your hands off of my fear! It's mine!" (Laughter) And you would battle to keep it.

But in truth, beloveds, step by step, each time you ask, the Holy Spirit takes more and more and if you must ask a thousand times a day, then so be it. But ask and willingly let go. The other thing...when you ask the Holy Spirit to take something from you, it is wise also to say, "Holy Spirit, please take this from me and please help me to *allow you* to take it. Help me to allow you to take it." Because many times, on the one hand you're giving and on the other hand you're pulling it back. So it is very important for you to be aware that you have to also ask for help to let it go.

Don't forget, beloveds, you have had this anger inside of you for thousands and thousands and thousands of years so it's not something you're going to get rid of in a twinkling but you do get rid of it. You do get rid of it and each time the Holy Spirit is called upon, *it* becomes more powerful, the ego becomes less powerful, and so it goes until finally, at last you discover that you are forgiven. Because you are forgiving, you are forgiven. And then the love of God comes flooding in upon you and it becomes your reality. It becomes your reality.

Have you anything to ask of me?

Participant: You had mentioned earlier about...you looked over here and you said, "I may not like what he says." And I [inaudible] agree, and so what I'm thinking is forgiveness vs. standing up for oneself. I have a little bit of a confusion about that.

Gabriel: Forgiveness is not passivity. It is not being passive and letting the world walk all up and down you. That's not forgiveness. Beloved woman, when you have a sense of self-worth, when you know that you are the child of God—not *the only* child of God and the rest of you poor slobs forget it...not that (laughter)—but when you know you are the child of God, you have a deep and abiding love and respect for yourself. So therefore, you are not going to allow anyone else to tarnish that.

So, when you *perceive* that another is attacking you, you have two choices. You can listen to the voice of the ego, which will say, "Slap him upside of the head," (laughter) or you can listen to the voice of the Holy Spirit, which will say to you, "The son of God cannot be harmed. This person is so in need of love that they feel they need to attack me. They fear so therefore they attack. I will love them out of their attack." And you do not take to heart what they are saying or doing because they are not attacking you. They are attacking themselves but like you, they have projected out *onto* you what they perceive to be a just reason for them to attack you. Really, they are attacking themselves so if they are attacking themselves, then think of the poverty of spirit they are in. They are not feeling loved at all by anyone, anywhere.

So, listening to the voice of the Holy Spirit, one would then say, "Dear Father, bless this soul. Bless this person. I send them love and I do not take unto myself the wrath of their words." And you let it go right on by.

Participant: Okay, so standing up for oneself really isn't standing up for oneself. It starts with...

Gabriel: That's right. Not in the terms of psh, psh, psh...get out of my face. Not that.

Participant: Well, like speaking up and saying, "Not true!"

Gabriel: Well, you could say to them, "Just a moment. I do not invite your words of anger. I care not to hear them, thank you." But on the higher level with the Holy Spirit, *there* is your power. There you bless and you *love* into *light* this poor wretch that feels they must attack you.

Participant: And because we're still learning to let it go, allow us to let it go, when it happens where we get that little...you know how it is...you just run into that person. You go, "Oh geez, I don't want to see that person." That's just another signal to let us know that it's still stuck in here then?

Gabriel: Ah, indeed. When you say, "Oh, I don't want to see that person," what you are really saying is, "I am refusing to look at the face of Christ." Now, does that mean you have to be around people who antagonize you and just grit your teeth and bear it? No. It means that you go with a higher purpose and that higher purpose removes the antagonism and you no longer perceive them as enemies or antagonists. You perceive them as a child of God, *very* lost indeed and very frightened.

Participant: Okay, all right. I have one other question here. It seems to me...this is more global, actually... There seems to be a proliferation of telling people, "If you've been injured by another person, go to these injury lawyers and we're going to get your money back," and I get like a bad feeling in the pit of my stomach. This is all over the televisions now. Hire these attorneys...

Gabriel: Simply don't listen.

Participant: Is it because of a wave of energy of opportunities to forgive? Is that why it's becoming so prevalent?

Gabriel: Yes, but it also... That consciousness has to fade away, beloved. This is why I am teaching this lesson tonight...is because as everyone learns forgiveness, there will be no attorneys on your earth. (Laughter)

Participant: So it's just coming up out of the dirt to be gotten rid of then. Okay.

Gabriel: You're not an attorney, are you? (Laughter)

Participant: No, I'm not. Beloved Gabriel, I just had a question. I wanted to follow up on what [she] said too about the person...of saying, "I don't want to encounter that person," or taking like a time-out from that person and then coming to the point and saying, "It really doesn't matter anymore."

Gabriel: Indeed, it doesn't matter.

Participant: When it doesn't matter anymore, do you make that person a part of your life? Do you just bless that person?

Gabriel: When it doesn't matter anymore, when you have come to the point where you have forgiven them totally and it really doesn't matter, most often that person just drifts out of your life and you don't have to deal with them anymore because you have released them. The only people you consistently have to deal with are the ones you hold to you in the antagonism and you *need* to forgive, and once you forgive them, two things happen. Once you forgive them, there develops a love between you, a Christ love between you. Then you don't mind being around them. Or, having fulfilled their purpose of antagonizing you to the point where you had to forgive them, they go out of your life. You don't need them there. They don't need to be there anymore so they are free to go.

Participant: Does the ego work through dreams?

Gabriel: Oh, the ego uses any methods it can get a hold of.

Participant: I have spoken with several people on the spiritual path who have had strange dreams this past month, old dreams that come up that I suppose would be fear-based, and in my own experience, I was wondering if it might be the ego at work because...I don't know.

Gabriel: Well, the ego will use any means, through fear, of getting to you. If they can throw you a nightmare or two that's going to knock your socks off, it will. It will. And remember, the ego always wants you to feel to blame. It always wants you to feel guilty and not worthy and anything that it can use to make you feel that way, it will use.

Participant: Okay. And I'm assuming it's also the ego if you have a day when you're just angry and you have no idea why you are angry, but you just don't want to look at anybody?

Gabriel: Then, beloved woman, when you have purposeless anger, that is being drawn to your attention as that which is within you which you need to forgive, release, and let go.

Participant: Forgive yourself.

Gabriel: Oh indeed, yes. This whole journey on your earth is all about being forgiven. By who? By you.

Participant: And you really don't have to know what it is you're ...

Gabriel: No. Would it be of any benefit to know that you once were part of the thundering hordes that went in and took over a country and slaughtered all the people and roasted little children and ate them with fruit and all that sort of thing? (Laughter)

Participant: No, because I don't think I would ever forgive myself.

Gabriel: Exactly. That is why...and by the way, you didn't do that, Tinker wants me to tell you. (Laughter) That is why the Holy Spirit is so precious, because the Holy Spirit *knows* the truth of you, that you *are* the child of God, but it also sees all the dreams that you make, the illusions and all the make-believes and it doesn't *believe that*. It believes the truth and it helps *you* to *know* the truth.

Participant: So the way out of this is to keep asking the Holy Spirit to help us.

Gabriel: To help you...and to forgive, forgive, forgive. Whoever. Whether it be a driver that cuts in front of you or someone from your past that beat the daylights out of you when you were little, it doesn't make any difference. The whole thing is to *release* them because in releasing *them*, *you* are released. *They* are the key to your freedom.

Participant: But that comes through the Holy Spirit.

Gabriel: Absolutely.

Participant: Why is there an ego?

Gabriel: Well, way back when you first decided to leave the kingdom of God within your consciousness, you created the ego as a method of protection. You believed you needed to be protected and therefore you needed an ally so you created this ego part of the personality that would warn you about things. It would say, "Oh, be careful of this. Watch out for that." It was meant to be your servant, but after a while it became your master because that was the only voice you heard.

Participant: Is your explanation of ego what I believe Satan to be or are we talking about two different things?

Gabriel: First of all, there is no Satan, but if you are of an orthodox belief system and you *believe* there is a Satan, I would say the ego would be equivalent to that, yes.

Participant: So there is no Satan?

Gabriel: No. Aren't you happy? (Laughter) With the ego afoot, you don't need a Satan. (Laughter)

Participant: You're saying that *we* created ego?

Gabriel: Yes, just as you created Satan. You had to have someone to blame for what you perceived to be your ill doings so you created this evil force that you named Satan and you said, "The devil made me do it." (Laughter)

Participant: And if I may, just one more question.

Gabriel: Indeed.

Participant: We've heard a lot about forgiveness. What happens when you don't forgive yourself and you die?

Gabriel: When you don't forgive yourself and you die? You come back to the earth to learn the same lessons over again and the same circumstances will present themselves to you for you to forgive and let go of. And you can do this as many thousands of times as you care to.

Participant: So my belief of when I die, I go to heaven or I go to hell ...

Gabriel: Well, there is no hell. I hate to tell you, but there is none.

Participant: When I die, if I have not forgiven myself, I will return to earth.

Gabriel: You will return and you will ...

Participant: And I will continue to have the same lesson over and over again until I forgive myself.

Gabriel: Indeed.

Participant: Once I *do* forgive myself and then I die?

Gabriel: And then you die? And then you rise up to... You see, beloved entity, you can only go in the heaven world where your *consciousness* takes you. In other words, if you are not aware of a blessing, it's as though the blessing isn't there. But when you become aware of the blessing, then the blessing seems to present itself when all the time it's been there all the while but you haven't seen it. And when you get to the spirit world, you will automatically go to where your consciousness is. If you believe in a heaven and hell, then you shall find a heaven and hell. If you believe in the forgiveness of God, then you will find forgiveness. If you believe that you can only go a certain way, then you will go a certain way.

You know, you have a joke upon the earth plane that is a grand truth as far as how people think. You have a joke where a Catholic died and went to heaven and a little while later a non-Catholic died and went to heaven. And Saint Peter directed him to the second door on the left and he said, "But please, do tiptoe past the first. The Catholics are in there and they don't know anyone else is up here." (Laughter) Now you see, your belief system will give you *exactly* what you expect when you reach the spirit world.

Participant: What's interesting to me is, from a counseling standpoint, it's always, "When you learn to love yourself, you can love others. When you can learn to accept yourself, you can accept others." But, if I'm not mistaken, you said, "As you forgive others, then you can forgive yourself."

Gabriel: Exactly right. Because, beloved woman, don't you see that nothing...no one has ever done anything wrong to anyone. But by the concepts of the masses, of the consciousness upon your earth, everybody's blaming someone for something. Everyone has an enemy of some sort or another. But the truth be that the only enemy lies within your own belief system. So, as you *forgive* these supposed enemies out there, who are you really forgiving? You're forgiving yourself.

Participant: So in the final analysis, you're really forgiving yourself and then you're able also to keep on forgiving everybody and not even seeing anything wrong in the first place to forgive.

Gabriel: Absolutely. Exactly.

Participant: When you have children who are teaseable and other children realize this and begin to harass them, what does that tell us about the teaseable child? Is that child an angry child?

Gabriel: It tells you that in that child's consciousness, it feels that the world is a scary, awful place to be and there are enemies out there that's going to get them. And what that child needs is to be assured that life is good, not frightening. Now, teach that child to listen for the sweet voice of the Holy Spirit, which tells the child the *good* things in life and *not* to listen to the other voice that says the world is a terrible place.

Participant: It must be very hard for this child to forgive the people who ganged up on him.

Gabriel: Perhaps, but then that child has asked for that opportunity to forgive. Do you have such a child?

Participant: No, I have no children.

Gabriel: But whether it be a child or whether it be an adult, it doesn't matter. The lesson is the same. In forgiving others, *you* are forgiving yourself.

Participant: Do we forgive them their stupidity and their foolishness? Is that what we are forgiving them for?

Gabriel: Forgiving yourself for stupidity and foolishness? Is that what you are asking? If you perceive that in others, then that's what you are seeing within yourself.

Participant: I mean, there are definitely hostile people who... I don't mean to turn this into too much of a person question.

Gabriel: But, beloved woman, do you not see that when you behold another as hostile, it is because the hostility is within you and you are projecting it *onto* that other person? You are saying *that* person is hostile to me, when in truth *you* are hostile to you, but because you don't see it that way, you see it as the enactment of another *against* you, when really...this is why this is this lesson tonight about forgiveness...is because until you recognize that the problem and the answer lies *within you*, you will *always* perceive that there are hostile people.

Participant: This bears a lot of thought. Thank you.

Gabriel: Indeed.

Participant: You talk about the two voices that we hear. Plenty of times I've tried to listen to those voices and figure out what is right, what is really the truth. Like you talk about how the ego tries to rationalize us to go with the ego. How do we discern between the two?

Gabriel: The ego is always the voice of fear. The ego will always sound a *warning* of some sort. The voice of the Holy Spirit is one of softness and sweetness. The Holy Spirit will gently lead you. Its voice is one of positive affirmation. It is a voice of comfort, "You are all right. You are all right." It is the voice that has no malice toward anything or anyone ever, under any circumstance. So when the voice teaches you something positive, that is the voice of the Holy Spirit. When there is fear involved or anger or anything of a negative nature, that is the ego.

Participant: So, if the voice is telling us, like a [inaudible] that something is good for us, then that would be the Holy Spirit?

Gabriel: If you are asking, "Is this good for me?" then you can know...just say, "Holy Spirit, guide me to my highest good." And then know that whatever action you take *is* for your highest good, even though it may not appear. Now, the Holy Spirit's purpose is to *teach you to forgive* and thus be forgiven. So, it will lead you into any situation that is going to teach you, offer you the opportunity of forgiveness.

So, when you say, "Guide me," that doesn't mean then the Holy Spirit is going to pick you up on a cloud and take you over the war zone and put you safely on the other side. However, what the Holy Spirit will do is present to you opportunity after opportunity after opportunity to forgive, to rise above, to forgive and rise above, to forgive and love, forgive and love, until finally you find out you have come through the war zone quite unscathed and you have learned ever so much.

Participant: In regards to our pot and all the thoughts that we aren't aware of that keep us from loving ourselves, would that be the main...would those thoughts be the main reason why we perceive that we can't manifest easily?

Gabriel: Oh indeed, yes, because that's the ego saying, "See, you can't do that. You don't have any power. You can't do that."

Participant: So even if we believe that, we can manifest and we proceed to use manifesting language that would manifest something for us, there are sort of sponsoring thoughts that are unknown to us?

Gabriel: Indeed. In the subconscious, there would be thoughts—belief systems rather than thoughts—that would say to you, "You really can't do this, you know. You really can't and I will prove to you because nothing's going to manifest."

Participant: And we may not be aware of it consciously.

Gabriel: And you're not aware of it. No, of course you're not.

Participant: You mentioned tonight about being angry with God. Did you say that that's a projection of our anger with ourselves because of our unwillingness to accept God's love?

Gabriel: Yes, and because you feel that you are not *worthy* of accepting God's love, you make it look like God is not loving *toward* you. You can say, "God doesn't love me. Look what a mess my life is in. If God loved me, He would take care of me," when all the while you are *rejecting* that care, rejecting that love, and saying, "I won't do what You want me to do, but see, You're the bad one." So, the anger really is toward yourself for *not* accepting the comfort and the love and peace of God.

Participant: And how about the feeling that you love God?

Gabriel: Well, you do love God. Everybody loves God. They just fight against it. Don't they beloved entity.

Participant: I wouldn't know. (Laughter)

Gabriel: Everyone loves God, beloved entity, but it is a scary...when you think, "Well, I love God," and you think, "but I don't think God loves me because..." So, it's kind of like you trick yourself into thinking that you love God but God doesn't love you back. But when you truly love God and when you truly know the love of God, there is such a feeling of peace, such a feeling that everything is right in my world. No matter how it appears, I know that I am safe in the hands of God, and there is a peacefulness in you so that the chaos around you doesn't affect you. It doesn't come inside.

Participant: Would you say you really can't love God in the true sense until you really love and forgive yourself, right?

Gabriel: I would say that's quite accurate. You project God as being out there. But when you truly love yourself, you recognize God is within you and that all the while you have been loving God, only you just didn't know it.

Participant: That's part of the whole illusion that the ego is weaving, this web of illusion all the time that we're trapped in.

Gabriel: That's part of the whole illusion. Absolutely. Yes, indeed.

Participant: As the pot gets stirred up as we're making progress, that's actually nice to hear because as those things come up, you think you're not making *any* progress but in fact you're making progress because it's getting stirred up. As it gets stirred up and these old things come flashing in front of you or things that you keep giving to the Holy Spirit aren't quite resolved, do you keep reaffirming, "I'm the Christ. I'm the Christ. I'm the Christ"?

Gabriel: "I am the child of God, beloved of God," and then you *forgive*, constantly forgive.

Participant: What you perceive to be outside sources?

Gabriel: Indeed, because you truly are forgiving yourself.

Participant: Another teacher on forgiveness has said a wonderful thing, I thought. He said, "The end result of forgiveness is celebration," and I think a lot of us still sometimes don't see forgiveness as something..."What's in it for me?" I am wondering if you could comment on the whole idea of celebration.

Gabriel: Celebration is almost a natural outcome, the natural follow-up of the forgiveness because the reason you celebrate is that you recognize that there *never* was anything to forgive after all and that everything flows in a *freedom*. You have a new sense of adventure because now you don't regard life as scary or in a way, "Well, I'd like to do that but ..." Instead, you seize opportunities. You go with the flow, as you say in your world, and there is a sense of adventure, a sense of peace, a sense of fullness in your life that is very enriching, and it is true because you have no enemies either without or within. And once the enemy within is gone, through forgiveness, the next natural thing you do is to celebrate, and that celebration is a form of grace that I shall speak about the next time we meet. We are going to talk about redeeming grace.

Well, if there are no other questions, I shall have a prayer with you and send you on your way.

O Thou Eternal Love
that sustains, creates, abides,
that brings forth new life moment by moment,
that sees no fault in anyone,
whose boundless mercies spill out
to renew and refresh and rebuild
that which was broken.

O Father of all light, Father of all life,
in gratefulness we rest in the peace that is You.
In harmony and in love
with one another and with You,
we find the joy in which we were created,
and for all of this we give You thanks, indeed.

The Importance of Meditation
June 6, 1993

Know you what cosmic consciousness be? It is the removal of your limited concepts of yourselves as separate from All-That-Is.

I have often asked you to live from the Lord God of your beings but in order for you to do that, you must first become well acquainted with the Lord God of your being. And so this night I will teach you how to do that in order that you might truly live rather than to struggle through your experiences.

The presence of God is everywhere. The presence of God is as real and as powerful in the physical forms that you have created as it is in its divine essence. The only difference is that it moves very, very slowly. And because it is ever behind the movement of the universe, the movement of that which is Spirit, it takes unto itself all of the heaviness and all of the negation that is being left behind by the cosmos.

And so this night I will teach you methods of freeing yourself from that, for there are those of you here who are suffering in the emotional plane. You are pained in your love life. There those of you here who are pained in your mental bodies because you are envisioning confusion and limitation. And there are those of you here who are ill in your physical bodies. And I desire greatly that when you leave this place this night that you be healed in every sense of that word.

The doorway to knowing God is the door though which you step when you meditate. I cannot emphasize to you enough the importance of daily meditation or communion with the divine, for it is only in that way will you leave behind you those things which hold you down, limit you, and cause you pain.

It matters not how frequently you pray; it matters greatly how frequently you meditate. Prayer is when you voice your needs. The Father has already known of your needs. Meditation is when you leave behind the need and enter into the answer, and I shall explain it this way.

First of all, let me explain that meditation has nothing to do with how religious you are. I care not what religion you have embraced throughout your life. That has nothing to do with any of what I am about to say to you.

When you meditate, you withdraw your attention from the five senses. Now, the five senses are the vehicles through which you operate while you are in your three-dimensional world. It is through these that you know what you see, hear, taste, touch, and feel. But the five senses will imprison you in your world of limitation, for from the five senses you *perceive* your limitations, you *perceive* your illnesses, you *perceive* those things which have gone awry in your lives. So therefore, to truly mediate, one pulls one's attention *from* the five senses.

Now you have entered into the realm of the emotional body, and that is your feeling nature. It is in the emotional body that you love or hate, that you know anger, that you feel distressed. So therefore, the emotional body would also bind you to your limitations. So one must withdraw from the emotional body. That is the most difficult body to withdraw from, for that is the one that clamors the loudest for your attention. That is the one that would have you believe that your whole world is there in your feelings, so one must go past it.

Now you withdraw up into the mental body and there you encounter conflicting thoughts. It is there that the mental body attacks your *journey*, for it fears for its life, so it will place into your mind all manner and form of limitation. Thoughts such as, "Instead of sitting here doing this, I should be out and about doing thus-and-so. I wonder if I left something turned on that should be turned off. I wonder if I remembered to do this or to do that. Have I forgotten to do such-and-such? Better I go and look." No. Better you say to the mental body, "Cease, be still, and do not impede my journey."

Now you leave behind the mental body and you enter into the essence of that which is you, your real, true self, your Spirit. To know God is to become aware of that essence, which is you, that has *nothing* to do with the physical body, *nothing* to do with your feelings, *nothing* to do with your thoughts.

When you leave behind these realms of limitation, you do not enter into that which is foreign to you or enter into that which is new to you. Rather, you have taken away the coverings—the veils, the sheaths, the coats, whatever you care to call it—of all of the illusions that you have created and you stand naked in the true aspect of yourselves.

Now, in your allegory of Adam and Eve, you will note that they became quite uncomfortable when they looked and discovered they were naked and they quickly sought to clothe themselves. Now, this is an allegory. This is a symbolism. When you first realized that you decided you could do without God, you sought to clothe and cover up that God aspect of you and so you clothed yourself with the mental body, with an emotional body, and ultimately, with physical form.

Now up unto that point, you *knew* God. You knew who you were. You had no problem with memory at all. You knew that you and the Father were one. You worshiped Him—It, Her, whatever you care to call It—in the truest sense of the word by the very *beingness* of what you are, and there was nothing that interfered with that worship. There was not a time set aside for worship or prayer, for all of you were at one with all of God. But when you decided to cover up that All-ness, you impeded your ability to be aware, totally absolutely aware, of God. Now, meditation is that journey back to that time when you are aware of your At-one-ment with God. And this is cosmic consciousness.

Meditation has been greatly misunderstood upon your earth plane. I have gone among you and I have watched those of you who meditate and I have noted that you keep track of a *good* meditation and one that is a *bad* meditation and the good ones you feel are few and far between and the bad ones have become sort of normal. Well, now I am going to break your balloon.

Meditation *cannot* be known by the physical body. True meditation cannot be known by the emotional body. It is totally beyond the mental body. It is nothing that you will bring in a conscious way and *judge* on any of those levels, for true meditation takes you *beyond anything* that the physical, emotional, or mental body could offer you. Meditation is not a thought, for you are beyond thought. It is not a feeling, for you are beyond feeling. It certainly is of nothing of the physical body. You are totally unaware of your body. Even if you were to be in pain, you would be unaware of it.

It is that moment when you are past *all* of the illusions that you live every day and it takes you beyond anything of the five senses, beyond anything of your feeling nature, beyond anything of your thought pattern. It is the emancipator. It is that which sets you free and brings you into your totalness.

Now, once having reached that state—with few exceptions, all of you here have at one point or another—when you return to your bodies, you bring back with you not a memory, for memory is an illusion, but a knowing. And I cannot tell you what that is like because you do not have any words that would adequately describe it, and I refuse to mislead you by saying it is something it is not. But you bring back with you that essence of is-ness and it touches into the mental body and in so doing, it quickens the mind. It draws the mind's attention *away from* that which is lesser than itself, which would be the emotional body and the physical body, and causes it to be colored, as it were, by that essence of divinity and in so doing, broadens your *knowingness*.

Now then, it filters into the emotional body of you. While it is in your mental body, it takes away anxiety, fear, confusion, the feeling of "I don't know what to do," the feeling of indecision. All of these things become lesser because they are not a truth and that which you have brought back with you *is* truth—pure, crystal truth—and so it *has to* eliminate that which is non-truth.

Now it comes into the emotional body. At that point, it takes away the illusion of separateness because the feeling of being separated is what causes you emotional pain. It is that which causes you to fancy that you are not loved. It is that which causes you to feel alone—loneliness, abandonment, bereft of any form of comfort. Anybody here not been there?

As it comes into that emotional body, it brings with it the profound feeling of *acceptance*, and that acceptance is born of *you*. You no longer concern yourself as to whether you are accepted by another. You *know* you are accepted by God and you accept yourselves because *you* are the only one who *cannot* accept yourself. It is impossible for another to not accept you; they are not you. So any feeling of rejection that you project out onto another is *your* rejection of yourself, and you perceive it to come *from* another person.

Now this that reaches down into your emotional body heals that feeling, for then you become aware of a profound sense of love and you perceive that profound sense of love as *being* within yourself. And guess who you love the most? You.

Now it comes down into the physical body and it heals the cells and the molecules of that body, for all that healing is, is the acceptance of divine love in every portion of your being.

Now, each time you meditate, you do this. Each time you go through these—releasing the body, releasing the feelings, releasing the mind—and going into that center of sacredness that is you, when you bring your awareness back into your three-dimensional world, you have been transformed.

Now, this is not a feeling that is going to suddenly burst upon you. It is a feeling that you gradually become aware of because it is a gentle flowing. It is a gentle cleansing. It is a gentleness that enwraps you and takes away all of the garbage that you have created and wrapped yourselves in. It releases the truth of you into your consciousness and that's the only thing that has separated you all this time...is your refusal to allow that truth of your being to become a conscious thing. On the one hand you pursue it ardently and on the other hand you flee from it.

Now, these meditations gently restore you to that state where every part of you becomes aware of God and in that awareness, you come to realize that *you* are what you have been seeking. I can see in the ethers over your heads that is a difficult thing for you to accept. Some of you are thinking that is self-worship and so forth. That is not what I'm talking about. I'm talking about removing the barriers that you have created that cause you to believe that you are separate from God.

Anybody here believe that God is not everywhere present? If He be everywhere present, then why isn't He present within you? And if He be present within you, coming to love *you* is coming to love God, is it not? Now think on this. This in no way takes away from the God of your past. It in no way depreciates the value of the Christ. If anything, it enhances it because it causes you to become aware of what you are within you.

In your meditations, there is no such thing as a bad meditation. There is no such thing as a meditation that doesn't bring you where you need to be. I go among you and I watch you shoot yourselves down time after time. I ask you, choose yet again to listen to the voice of God within you.

Daily meditation is the most valuable spiritual truth that you can live, for only in that will you come to know the Father and thusly to know yourselves. As your limitations fall away, and they will, you will realize that, as I have ever taught you, knowing God is the simplest thing. It is just a matter of letting go of all of the reasons you have created why you shouldn't know Him, and you have created a lot of fancy things, I can tell you. Some of them are absolutely hilarious. Others are sad. But they are all illusions, every one.

Now, I have been among you, I and those of my kind, and we have noted that the past month of your earth time has been rather horrendous, has it not? Anyone here escaped the maladies of, "Oh my God"? (Laughter) Nowhere that I've been. Now, you each have dealt with these things in the most profound of human manner, out and out panic. (Laughter) I've watched you.

Now, here's what you do. This coming month you will meet some more "Oh, my God's" and here is what you do. When they present themselves—and I care not what form they take or where you are when they attack you—you take that moment and you close your eyes and you go up to your Source. You leave behind the physical that would tell you all kinds of erroneous things. You leave behind your feeling nature, which will be *screaming* at you. You leave behind your mental body that's going to be racing about saying, "What if, what if, what if, what if. Oh my God, what are we going to do? This is awful. This is awful. Emotional body get up and run! We're out of here!"

You go up to that silent place and you make your connection, and it's so simple to make that connection. You simply go there and you say, "Thank you, my God, for being one with me now," and you bring that back with you. And as you come into your mental body, you say to it, "Peace, be still." There is nothing that you can think that is not of God, and all that you think this moment is transformed into that which is good.

Then you come into your emotional body who by this time is totally hysterical. Did you know that all the emotional bodies are feminine?

Participant: I'm not surprised. (Laughter)

Gabriel: You've got to go home with her. You're dead meat! (Laughter) Well, you joke, but I'll tell you why they are...I mean it...they are feminine and I will tell you why. I know you are all thinking, "Because women go hysterical," but I've seen some hysterical men too. As a matter of fact, you don't do bad at hysterics. (Laughter)

Now, your emotional body is that which is sustaining. It is that which is nurturing in you. It is that which loves, holds, sustains, caresses, uplifts, and so therefore, it *has* to be feminine. Now, this does not take away from the masculinity of the male gender, lest you be fearful that it will, but it doesn't at all. But because it is sustaining, it also is sustaining of negative feelings and that is why you can change your mind but it is more difficult to change your feeling nature. Have you ever noticed that? You can change your thinking pretty much like that, but when you get into the emotional body, it's saying, "I don't *want* to change. This is *not* what I'm supposed to be doing. If I leave this feeling of despair, it will die!" (Laughter) And so you go back to your feelings of despair and you nurture them.

But when you get to the emotional body, the first thing you must say to it is, "I love you. The God of me treasures you," and in that love you are healed and all that you feel is perfect love. Now this has a calming, quieting effect upon the emotional body, for at once it is wrapped in the love of God and there it is secure, and so it will bring forth all of that security in its givingness, in its sustainingness.

Now you bring this into the physical body and you say to your nervous system—for your nervous system is the conductor of your psychic energy, don't forget that—you say to your nervous system, "Be still, be calm, for all is well. You are loved. You are at peace and there is nothing for you to be upset about." Allow this feeling to come over you and you will find as you do this, each time you do it, it is something that just sort of happens because what you are doing is using your *true nature*. You are using that element of Spirit that is God within you, and you are dealing with whatever your circumstances be *from that point*.

Now, what is going to happen? Your physical body becomes calm. The adrenalin slows down. The heartbeat becomes normal. Your breathing becomes relaxed. The cells of your body lose all of their destructive forces and become *con*structive again, and instead of producing headaches and upset tummies and all that sort of thing, you are producing good health, vitality, physical strength, and endurance.

In the emotional body, anxiety disappears. There's no more feelings of, "Oh dear, what shall I do?" Instead, there is a sense of perfect calm and in that calmness, the mental body of you can think positive thoughts. It is now open and receptive for the inflow of divine ideas and instead of racing around and frantically saying, "I know not what to do," there comes into your knowingness clear instructions. It is something that you will instinctively know and you will calmly, and with a certainty, go forth to take whatever action is required.

And do not be surprised if it is required to take *no* action. Remember, "Be still and know that I am God." And frequently, the most powerful thing that you can do is do is do nothing. Remember that, for all of you are of a nature to rush out and *do* something. Sometimes it is best to just be still and wait.

Being still and waiting serves many purposes. For one thing it prevents you from making a monkey of yourself. On a more concrete note, it allows the helpful forces that surround you, the angels if you will, to *do* a miracle for you because you're not in the way.

[To a participant] You have a great track record for knocking miracles [inaudible], did you know that? We get one all set to send your way and you give it a kick in the butt and away it goes.

Sometimes in your stillness is where most of your power lies. Don't forget that. There is a saying you have upon the earth, "When in doubt, do nothing." And that is a great truth. Simply wait.

Participant: Gabriel, in our meditation, when we meditate, if we go to sleep and then we wake up, is that part of the meditation too or no?
Gabriel: No.
Participant: Just the part where you are not asleep.
Gabriel: The part where you are awake.

Participant: If we start out to meditate and we only get to the part where, or we get to a part where we're aware of the fact that we think the phone might ring or something else happens and we don't get beyond that point, we haven't really been meditating? Is that what you're saying?
Gabriel: When you become interrupted, it is because you have set yourself up to be. There are ways of meditating without interruption. Choose your times well when you *know* you will not be interrupted.

Participant: Okay, so that we haven't really been meditating if we haven't gotten beyond that one point?
Gabriel: No. Indeed.

Participant: If we have a question about what is truth, can we find the answer in meditation?
Gabriel: Indeed, you can. Indeed, you can.
Participant: How will the answer come?
Gabriel: It will come within your knowingness. It will not come as a voice in your ear or anything. It will just come in your knowingness. It may be that several days of your perceived time will pass before the answer is there, but something will trigger it and you will say, "Ah yes, now I know."

Participant: I always want to say, "Hi," and that just feels so trite. I don't know what to say to you. Hi. (Laughter)
Gabriel: Hi to you too! (Laughter)
Participant: I felt like your lecture today was particularly relevant and I want to thank you for that. I've experienced my meditations the way you've described it, where at the time, it wasn't this grand capsule bursting but when I came back to my awareness, certain junk that I created in my life...it just became so clear that it was junk. It was just so clear to me that it was junk and that I created it and there was no reason for it.
Gabriel: Indeed.
Participant: And my state of being during my meditation was that was pure and right and that was what I should bring back to my awareness with me all

the time. And I really felt that as you were talking about that.

Gabriel: Indeed.

Participant: You said something that was really important to me today. You said, "Sometimes in your stillness is where most of your power lies." I have trouble with that.

Gabriel: Most people in the physical body *do* have trouble with it because you are trained from little ones to *do* something to make something right.

Participant: Well, in this day and age, we're also learning to create and use affirmations and all of that good stuff and I have trouble finding the balance line between putting out my energy and being still and allowing. I have trouble finding the balance between that. Can you say something to help me clear that up?

Gabriel: When there is the feeling within you of uncertainty, when you are not clear on what action is appropriate, then is the instruction to be still. You don't always have to do something for something to right itself. Frequently, situations left alone will right themselves much more quickly.

Participant: You mentioned getting past the physical, the mental, and the emotional/mental and into the spiritual. Would it be a good idea to use a mental step with the love affirmations you gave us? Will that bring us past those steps? Because I've meditated and I know that sometimes I haven't gotten past the emotional. Will that calm it?

Gabriel: When you use an affirmation in your meditation, if you desire to use one, use it in the beginning of it and then leave it be, for while you are saying an affirmation, you are keeping your mental body extremely active and while it is active, you're not going to go past it. If you are reciting something within yourself, your mental body is what is forming the thoughts and you're not going to get past it. It's like trying to cross a street when all of the modes of transportation are bumper to bumper going the other way. So to go past the mental body is to still it. Now, you will never be without thought but you do not *engage* the thoughts. Let them drift. Do not follow after them. As a thought comes into your mind, allow it to pass and just keep going.

Participant: And it will be clear?

Gabriel: It will be clear.

Participant: You must have told us before and I missed it, that the emotional body was to be loved.

Gabriel: Oh, indeed.

Participant: That it was a nurturing part of us and I guess I always got it that it was in the way and we had to get rid of it because it does ...

Gabriel: Oh no. No, it is the coat. It is the instrument that your feeling nature uses. Your emotional body is the vehicle for your feeling nature. It is *not* your feeling nature any more than your brain is your mind. The brain is the instrument *for* the mind. The emotional body is the instrument for the feeling nature of you. Your mental body is the vehicle that your knowingness uses when being brought down into concrete thought, so your emotional body is precious indeed.

141

Participant: So, if we start treating it as a precious thing rather than something in the way...

Gabriel: Well, you've got to stop kicking its backside sometime. You have to embrace it and love it for what it is, a *vehicle* for your feeling nature.

Participant: Thank you. That clarifies a lot of things.

Gabriel: Now you can get out the Band-Aids and patch it all up, eh? (Laughter)

Participant: I've had several "Oh, my God" experiences this past month.

Gabriel: I know.

Participant: I was taking notes on going up to the silent place and making connection. You had given us a list of things to say to the emotional body and I didn't get them all. If you could give them again.

Gabriel: What have you got?

Participant: Go to the emotional body and say, "I love you."

Gabriel: Indeed. Tell it you love it. Tell it there is no reason for it to be so distressed, that all that is coming into it is the love of God and that will sustain all things. Anything to that effect. You don't have to use my words exactly. Whatever would calm your emotional body for you. Three words are sufficient if you say them with enough conviction, "Peace, be still." That will calm anything.

Participant: Any time that I ever try to meditate, I start with the same feeling and I end with the same feeling and that's just a complete blank. I get absolutely nothing. It's zero. I don't see anything. I don't think about anything. I just am hollow like.

Gabriel: That is wondrous!

Participant: I am meditating, am I?

Gabriel: Indeed you are! Now, do not be misled. In meditation, you are not supposed to *see* something necessarily or hear something. That's of the five senses. But when you are blank, it is because you have transcended. You have gone up past all of the things I've just said—the physical, the mental, the emotional, and so forth—and you have touched into it.

Participant: But I do it immediately and my five emotions are dead.

Gabriel: You have gone past them. They're not dead. They're not dead. You have just slipped past them and that is all right.

Participant: Then I probably end up going to sleep. I don't know what happens. (Laughter)

Gabriel: Try not to go to sleep, for when you do that, you are not in control then. Then you are out of your body and you are not in control. But when you are awake and in this state where it seems to be blank to you, that is all right. There's nothing wrong in that. You will be amazed at what you are bringing back with you. Just because you have no conscious mind of it doesn't mean it isn't there.

Participant: I was wondering if it would be better to meditate twice a day as opposed to once a day?

Gabriel: Oh indeed, twice a day is always best. Early in the morn and in the evening, *not* when you are going to bed for then you are thinking of sleep, but before that.

Participant: About how long should you meditate? Is there a feeling that accompanies when you're through? Is it a knowingness?

Gabriel: There is and I'm not...I have to ask because I don't know your time. Ten minutes, whatever that be. (Laughter)

Participant: Could you elaborate on why we get our headaches?

Gabriel: Why you get your headaches?

Participant: Headaches. You were mentioning that it comes from the emotional body. Why is it that we manifest that?

Gabriel: When you have your headaches, as you perceive it to be, it is because you have allowed your mental body to become so congested with old stuff, as it were, that when it comes into the brain part of you, it expands the cells and they get uncomfortable in your skull. Now, you also can do this at the bottom of your neck. There is a thing there...I don't know what you call your...there is a gathering there of nerves and when you are so tense in your mental body, that tension is brought down into the nervous system and there is a tightening there and this causes a pressure which causes pain. A person who is very...what do you call it? Laid down...laid away...

Someone: Laid back.

Gabriel: Laid back...is usually very unlikely to have headaches because they are so relaxed all the time. People who are tense, they are the ones with the headaches, and ladies at certain times of the month. (Laughter)

Participant: So to clear up our headaches is to allow the mental junk that we've collected...to allow it to pass.

Gabriel: Just allow it to go from you.

Participant: Thank you for being here. Since everyone is asking about sleep, I have a question about sleep. There is something that is known as "astral travel" that we speak of here and I would like to know if you can explain that and if it indeed exists.

Gabriel: Oh indeed, it does exist. First of all, the physical body...the physical...the earth is not your natural habitat, so you stay here only a certain length of time and then every part of you longs to return home. Since you cannot pass away every night, as it were—well, you could, but it wouldn't work too well—what happens is that you withdraw from your physical body without severing the cord that attaches into the solar plexus and keeps you attached to your body. You withdraw, remaining attached by that cord, and then you just travel wherever you will. That cord is very elastic. It stretches quite far.

About the only thing you *don't* do is to go past a plane where the vibration is so fine that you couldn't manifest on it in your astral body. Have I answered you?

Participant: Yes.

Gabriel: Now, the astral body is of a certain vibration and will vibrate only on the astral plane. You cannot take your astral body into the mental plane because it simply wouldn't...the vibrations there would be very uncomfortable for it. So it travels about the astral plane.

Now, the astral plane is a very vast, limitless place to be. You can go to the lower part, which is dark and not pleasant at all, or you can go up to the higher astral where it is very wondrous indeed. So you travel wherever you choose.

That is where your dreams come from. That is what you perceive to be dreaming...is your travels on the astral plane.

Participant: I want to ask you about crying as a way of letting go of physical tensions that you've held in and emotional tensions.

Gabriel: Crying is a release but it should not be the only way, the only method you use, because chronic crying, after a while...for one thing, you will harm your physical body. And not that only, but that is not the...then it is no longer an answer. Then it becomes a problem. Tears of anger, tears of frustration, tears of sorrow are certainly welcome for a time but when that time is over, then the tears should cease.

Participant: What harm could you do to your physical body?

Gabriel: I don't know. Let me ask. You have little...ducks, you have ducks? Chickens? (Laughter) Just ducks.

Someone: Tear ducts.

Gabriel: [Looking in someone's eyes] That is rather amazing. Ah, there they be. All right. That can become inflamed and either become so inflamed that you develop a kind of a disease behind the eyes because of it. So you *can* harm your body.

Isn't it interesting you have little "ducks" there. I thought they were creatures with feathers. (Laughter)

Someone: They are spelled differently. D-U-C-K-S is the animal. D-U-C-*T*-S in the one in your eye.

Gabriel: And that is a difference... (Laughter)

Someone: They sound the same.

Gabriel: All right.

Participant: Gabriel, I never thought of this before but you always talk about how when we leave this plane, we'll go to the astral and then up through the various planes, but *you* don't go through all these planes when you...?

Gabriel: I do but I am usually not...they are not aware of me because of my vibration.

Participant: So you have to come through the astral plane?

Gabriel: Oh, indeed.

Participant: So you don't go to the dark part of the astral plane.

Gabriel: Occasionally I do to assist someone.

Participant: Hi Gabriel.

Gabriel: You are back again.

Participant: Oh, you remember me. (Laughter) I just have a question actually I'm rather concerned about because I've been meditating a certain way for many, many years now and in listening to you, it seems as though I might be doing it wrong because I meditate with a mantra that I repeat over and over throughout the entire time. And you're talking about getting out of the *mental* and that's very mental. So I'm wondering, is it inappropriate that I meditate that way?

Gabriel: Mantras are very useful for those who are new to meditation but after meditation has become a habit to you, the mantra would tend to keep you centered in your mental body. You may use it for a moment or two in the beginning to get yourself started, but then it is best to release it.

Participant: Okay, so I can still use it at the beginning to get me to that place where it gets me to and then...

Gabriel: Indeed.

Participant: So this is new. So now, all of a sudden, I'm going to spend the whole time not focusing on that mantra (laughter) but rather...what do I do? Just create like a blank?

Gabriel: No, no. Do not create. When you create, you are engaging your mental body in activity, for it is through the mental body that you create. When you have said your mantra and you have passed up through the mental body, as you feel the mantra leave you—and you will feel it leave you—do not call it back nor do you... Mantras are useful in this way. It prevents the mind from wandering and bringing in foreign matter, as it were, for the mind is centered on the mantra. Now, that is a divine intent. After a bit, the essence of the divine intent should take over and the use of *word* becomes undesirable. Know you what I say?

The mantra...each of you has a certain mantra that is given to you because of its vibratory rate being in harmony with *your* vibratory rate. Very few people have the same mantra or they have a derivative of it and it is different, a different tone, whatever. Now, that is given to you to harmonize your centers, to bring you into harmony and into a singleness of purpose. Now, that is the essence, the intent of it.

Now, the intent of it is very wondrous indeed, but a lot of students get caught up in the *mantra* and become *solid* in *it* and feel if they do not have their mantra, "Oh, I cannot meditate. I do not have my mantra." Now, the object of meditation is to go past *all* limitation, including that of the mantra. So once you have used the mantra to bring you up to that mental, you will feel the mantra go from you. Allow it to be so and just keep going.

I must leave you with a...oh, come forth. I will answer one more.

Participant: I have a question about astral travel. How can one consciously go into...
Gabriel: I'm looking at your "ducks." (Laughter) I wondered if they be different because you wear appendages on your face, but they are the same.
Participant: They are the same.
Gabriel: Indeed. Thank you.
Participant: You're welcome. About astral travel, how can I...if dreams are our astral travels, is there a way to bring either... make a conscious effort to decide before...consciously decide where we *want* to go on the astral plane and work to bring that back to our consciousness? Is that necessary and/or is it possible to take...to simply...obviously, your subconscious or

your other part of you that travels when you sleep *knows* where to go?

Gabriel: You *can* direct yourself. You can say, "I desire greatly to go to a certain place," and then you will go there. You will go there. You may not consciously remember it, especially if it is a place that your reasoning mind feels is useless, but you can go anywhere you choose.

Participant: Just will it.

Gabriel: Just will it.

Now I am to close. Indeed. Well, I bless all your little "ducks." (Laughter) And I shall close with a prayer.

Divine Essence,
oh Thou Great Holiness that is life,
how thankful I am for this exchange
with these, Thy beloveds.
How thankful I am to serve this Holiness,
this Sacredness that is You.

For all that is
and all that we are privileged to know,
I give You thanks
and I know that this Holiness
is becoming an active awareness
in the beingness of these whom Thou lovest so.
So be it.

And I shall see you again.

Index

Index

Index

Index

Index

About the Author

Reverend Penny Donovan, a natural medium since childhood, was ordained in 1960 at the John Carlson Memorial Institute in Buffalo, NY. She obtained her Doctor of Divinity degree from the Fellowships of the Spirit in Buffalo, NY. In 1964 Rev. Penny founded the Trinity Temple of the Holy Spirit Church in Albany, NY, and served as the pastor there for thirty years. In 1994 she retired from that position to devote full time to spreading the teachings of Archangel Gabriel whom she had channeled from 1987 to 1999. Since Gabriel's departure, Rev. Penny has continued teach and conduct spiritual healing sessions in classes and retreats.

Made in the USA
Middletown, DE
18 August 2021

46277211R00102